DATA TEAMS:
The Big Picture

Looking at Data Teams
Through a Collaborative Lens

DATA TEAMS:
The Big Picture

Looking at Data Teams
Through a Collaborative Lens

Elle Allison | Laura Besser | Lauren Campsen
Juan Córdova | Brandon Doubek | Linda Gregg
Connie Kamm | Kris Nielsen | Angela Peery
Barb Pitchford | Ainsley Rose
Stephen Ventura | Michael White

With a Foreword from Douglas B. Reeves, Ph.D.

The Leadership and Learning Center
317 Inverness Way South, Suite 150
Englewood, Colorado 80112
Phone 1.866.399.6019 | Fax 303.504.9417
www.LeadandLearn.com

Published by Lead+Learn Press, a division of Advanced Learning Centers, Inc.

ISBN 978-1-933196-99-2

Printed in the United States of America

14 13 12 11 10   01 02 03 04 05 06 07

Contents

List of Exhibits

About the Authors

Dr. Elle Allison is a Senior Professional Development Associate with The Leadership and Learning Center. She is also the founder of Wisdom Out—an organization devoted to bringing the practice of wisdom off the mountain and putting it into the hands of people everywhere. She is recognized in education for her knowledge and expertise in working with individuals, teams, and organizations to provide students with masterful learning opportunities in standards-based classrooms and systems.

Laura Besser is the Director of Content and a Senior Professional Development Associate with The Leadership and Learning Center. She is a lifelong educator and truly believes that all students, teachers, and leaders can succeed. She embraces results, holds high expectations, and engages educators to build on their strengths. Her teaching experience spans many levels and environments. As an instructional coach, she skillfully guided teachers to improved professional practices. As an adult educator and literacy consultant, she was able to share experiences, best practices, and research to further impact teaching and learning in the classroom. In her role as principal, she combined all of her rich experiences and knowledge into transforming teaching and learning.

Lauren Campsen is a Professional Development Associate for The Leadership and Learning Center and also is the principal of Ocean View Elementary School in Norfolk, Virginia. In 2008, Ocean View was recognized by the U.S. Department of Education as a national No Child Left Behind Blue Ribbon School. In addition, the school was also recognized as a Distinguished Title I School in 2009 and 2010. In 2008, Ms. Campsen received the Terrell H. Bell National Principal Award for Leadership.

Juan Córdova is a Professional Development Associate at The Leadership and Learning Center. As a former ELL student, he dedicated his career as a teacher and administrator to working extensively with students who shared the same struggles that he did as a child. He would like to especially thank the children of Marion Oaks, Florida, for helping him build a community of learners.

Dr. Brandon Doubek is a Professional Development Associate for The Leadership and Learning Center who brings more than twenty years of experience to his work as a leader, teacher educator, professor, instructional strategy consultant, and researcher. He has provided seminars and follow-up site visits for Common Formative Assessments, Engaging Classroom Assessments, Data Teams, Decision Making for Results, Advanced Data-Driven Decision Making, Powerful Strategies for Effective Teaching, Writing to Learn, Response to Intervention, Differentiated Instruction, and Daily Disciplines of Leadership. He is known for engaging participants and students through humor and breaking down complex ideas into manageable pieces of information that can easily be implemented.

Dr. Linda Gregg is a Professional Development Associate with The Leadership and Learning Center. She is also the Director of Education for a residential treatment center in New Mexico. Dr. Gregg holds professional credentials in general education, special education, and school administration. She has taught elementary through high school grades and served as the principal of both elementary and high schools. She is a former Associate Superintendent of Federal Programs and Assistant Professor and Coordinator of the Special Education Program at the College of Santa Fe in New Mexico. Dr. Gregg is recognized for her expertise in working with diverse learners and bridging the achievement gap for students in special education.

Dr. Connie Kamm is a Senior Professional Development Associate with The Leadership and Learning Center. She is also the president of The KAMM Group, a consulting company that focuses on organizational development and alignment in both education and industry. Dr. Kamm has been active in school reform for more than twenty-five years and has developed keen insights into the spirit of building positive school cultures. She is noted for her dynamic process for educational change and facilitates systemwide, comprehensive accountability frameworks at state and district levels.

Dr. Kris Nielsen is a Professional Development Associate with The Leadership and Learning Center. She also teaches as an adjunct at the University of Minnesota in licensure programs for school administrators. Currently, she teaches a Data-Driven Decision Making class for aspiring school leaders. Dr. Nielsen works with schools nationally and internationally on issues of school improvement, assessment, instructional strategies, planning, and the effective use of data to improve school processes and instruction. She coaches principals and teachers in effective planning and in quality implementation of research-based practices.

Dr. Angela Peery is a Senior Professional Development Associate representing The Leadership and Learning Center in more than 100 speaking and consulting engagements per year. She is also the author of four books, including *Writing Matters in Every Classroom* (2009). In Dr. Peery's tenure at The Center, she has worked alongside dozens of Data Teams and building administrators to increase academic achievement.

Barb Pitchford is a Professional Development Associate with The Leadership and Learning Center and a veteran educator with more than thirty-five years of experience as a teacher, counselor, and administrator in K–12 public education. With nearly two thirds of her career as a building administrator, she understands the overwhelming and unrelenting challenges of the principal. She has become a passionate coach and consultant to principals and teacher leaders, understanding the multiple demands, guiding the change process, and sharing the belief that in the field of education, leaders must be the lead learners.

Ainsley Rose is a Professional Development Associate for The Leadership and Learning Center. As the former director of education and curriculum for the Western Quebec School Board in Gatineau, Quebec, he was responsible for initiating many systemic changes that continue to impact teaching and learning within the school board today. Throughout his career as an education leader, he has incorporated his expertise within a wide range of principles, practices, and concepts, all of which have significantly improved schools. He has presented across Canada and the United States on a range of educational topics.

Stephen Ventura is a Professional Development Associate for The Leadership and Learning Center. He is a highly motivational and knowledgeable speaker who approaches high-stakes data collection and decision making armed with practical, research-based strategies. He is a former elementary, middle school, and high school teacher. His administrative experiences encompass those of assistant principal, principal, director, and superintendent.

Dr. Michael White is a Professional Development Associate with The Leadership and Learning Center and the Director of Educational Consulting Services, an educational organization in Cincinnati, Ohio. He is also a licensed pediatric psychologist. Dr. White consults with school systems throughout the country on issues relating to new teacher training, standards-based instruction, and formative assessment. He is the author of four books and numerous articles on standards, assessment, and effective schools.

The Human Factors of Data Analysis

DOUGLAS B. REEVES, Ph.D.

Despite our elegies to the value of teaching, what do our professional development programs and practices really say about our respect—or lack of it—for teachers and administrators?

While schools around the world have more data than ever before, the use of the data to improve learning, teaching, and leadership remains inconsistent. The authors of this volume offer practical insights to help teachers, administrators, and policymakers cross the bridge from the theoretical capabilities of data systems to practical applications in classrooms. The authors of the chapters that follow bring a rich diversity of experiences and perspectives to their task, considering the needs of a wide range of students and schools. In these pages, you will find guidance for the most challenged schools that are struggling with student literacy and help for the most successful schools that are committed to continuous improvement in the twenty-first century.

I would like to offer a few "lessons learned" from the first decade of the twenty-first century. While our computers may be faster and cheaper today than they were ten years ago, data systems that are abundant and cheap are of little value if we do not take into consideration the human systems that remain vulnerable and complex. The lessons on the human side of data analysis come from three fictional characters—Mr. Spock, Huck Finn, and Madame Michel.

Just a few minutes watching the characters on the bridge of *The Starship Enterprise* allowed viewers to understand that Mr. Spock was devoid of emotion and fully committed to logic. But as Spock only occasionally learned, logic in a world dominated by humans is subject to emotional reactions. No matter how cool, calm, and rational school data analysts are, no matter how sophisticated their equipment, no matter how penetrating their insights, all of their energies are wasted if they fail to consider the emotional context of their conversations. While the intended message may be, "Some of our students need to perform better in reading and math," the received message is likely to be, "You are calling me an ineffective teacher and you have no idea of the realities of my classroom." From such beginnings, few productive discussions will follow.

When Huck Finn was musing about heaven, he considered the likely activities—praying and singing hymns—to be a punishment rather than a reward. "If that ain't hell," Huck mused, "I don't know what is." However well intentioned the gentle widow who was concerned with Huck's eternal soul, her admonitions fell on deaf ears. Similarly, many advocates of data in schools assume that the case for wonders of data is self-evident. Who wouldn't want to go to data heaven? Quite a few people. If "data" mean nothing more than a compilation of test scores once a year in an exercise many months removed from the actual student performance, then a substantial number of educators are understandably less than enthusiastic about the process. If "data" are only about student test scores and not also about systematic observations about teaching and leadership decisions, then they are as meaningful as studying the weight of students without considering diet and exercise. As any careful reader of Samuel Clemens knows, Huck was clever and intelligent. He did not automatically accept the enthusiasms of others just because they were earnest, sincere, and relentless—qualities all attributable to advocates of data analysis. Before we jump into the *how* of data analysis, we must take pains to think through with our colleagues the *why*—not only how analysis leads to improved scores, but how it influences the lives of students, families, and communities. Angry and alienated teachers and administrators can learn about data systems, but it is unlikely that people of these emotional dispositions will really use those systems.

In Muriel Barbery's *The Elegance of the Hedgehog*, the building concierge, Madame Michel, is a brilliant scholar and polymath, conversant in the most challenging works of philosophy and science. Yet, because she is a concierge, almost no one recognizes her wit and intellect. I am disheartened to see how many professional development programs devoted to data analysis appear to have as their first premise that teachers and administrators are incompetent. It is always interesting how our messages and delivery are often in conflict. We deliver lectures about the importance of "differentiated instruction" in precisely the same way to the same group. We require people to write dissertations on the value of collaborative learning without collaborating with other writers—that would be cheating.

And we deliver sermons on the value of data analysis without having first gathered data on the parishioners forced to listen to that particular preacher.

It is noteworthy that this foreword contains not a single number. Before we get to the numbers, we need to embrace the human side of data analysis. Spock was perplexed that people were emotional; we need not be. Huck was unwilling to accept uncritically the enthusiasm of others about the Pearly Gates; we dare not assume that everyone shares our view of the value of data. The neighbors of Madam Michel could not see the brilliance in front of them because of their stereotypes about the role, uniform, and social place of a building concierge. Despite our elegies to the value of teaching, what do our professional development programs and practices really say about our respect—or lack of it—for teachers and administrators?

Data systems are more sophisticated than ever before, and with the help of people like the authors in this book, we can use those systems to improve learning, teaching, and leadership. But at every turn, we must recall that we are working with people—people who have emotions, people who are smart, and people who are worthy of our respect. With that as a framework for a discussion of data analysis, you will more likely be able to apply the lessons of this book.

Nahant, Massachusetts
May 2010

What Are Data Teams?

LAURA BESSER

Data Teams are the single best way to help educators and administrators move from "drowning in data" to using information to make better instructional decisions. What makes the Data Teams process distinctive is that we are not just looking at student scores, but at the combination of student results, teaching strategies, and leadership support. The essential question is, "What can we do tomorrow to help students and teachers achieve their goals?" Data Teams give professionals respect, reinforcement, and feedback—the keys for improved impact on student learning.

DOUGLAS REEVES, 2010

Data Teams are collaborative teams designed to improve teaching, learning, and leadership. Most of us have been a member of a collaborative team of some sort. In our younger years we may have been members of chess clubs, glee clubs, soccer teams, or tennis teams, and as adults we may have indulged in the more "serious" team sports of bowling, fantasy football, and Nintendo Wii. As professional educators, we've all engaged in team-building activities such as ropes courses, retreats, and reflections. While these experiences may have taught us to work more efficiently through collaboration, perhaps to adhere to team norms, and to develop trust and respect—most likely these experiences alone did not have a great impact on student learning.

As educators, we've been asked to look at binders, files, and Web sites full of data. We have dutifully participated in "data days" where we sift through a bunch of student achievement numbers and try to make sense of it all. While this is a valuable activity, it's often not repeated until the following August. And if that's the case, we are often looking at numbers that represent learners who are no longer students at our schools and at learning that occurred months ago. While looking at data is a powerful practice, if it's not deliberate, frequent, and systematic, it won't have a dramatic impact on student achievement.

Collaboration is an effective practice and a thread of all data-driven decisions. Using data is an effective practice and, when used through collaboration, it allows us to get "beyond the numbers." Collaboration and use of data are independent practices, but they are also interdependent practices.

Data Teams were created when The Leadership and Learning Center married two powerful practices: professional collaboration and data-driven decision making. This union is one that is embedded in research and designed for results.

"Professional Learning Communities are what we are; Data Teams are what we do." This is a phrase used by many of our colleagues. As Professional Learning Communities, we are groups of educators who teach the same course, or grade level, or who have a similar focus. We can sit around the table and talk about student learning because we've also used the same formative assessment to measure student learning. We have common understandings of proficiency levels, and we share high expectations for all students in our classrooms. As Data Teams, we use a systematic process to look at student learning and student evidence. We use a "decision making for results" process in our Data Teams. This process allows us to have evidence-based conversations on teaching and learning. This five-step process, with an added sixth step of monitoring and evaluating, is embedded into each Data Teams meeting.

The Data Teams Process for Results

The Data Teams process encompasses five steps, as shown in Exhibit I.1. A "sixth step" involves monitoring and evaluating all of the results from Steps 1 through 5.

Data Teams: The Big Picture is a compilation of the many aspects, or lenses, of the Data Teams process. Each lens provides a different view of the Data Teams process and gives practical advice for implementation. While each chapter will offer you insight into the Data Teams process, the entire book will give you the Big Picture of the results-driven process we call Data Teams.

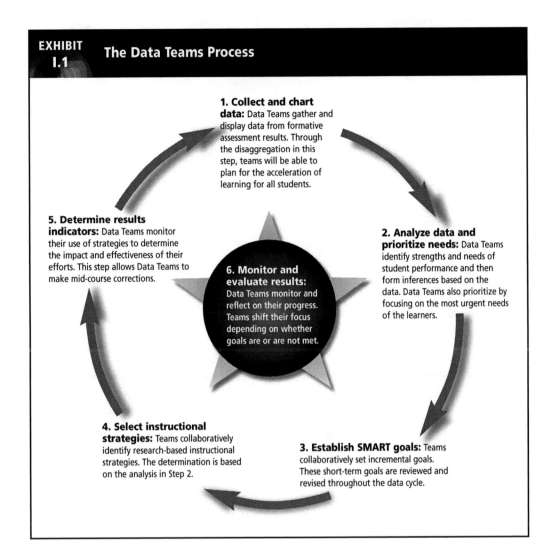

EXHIBIT I.1 The Data Teams Process

1. Collect and chart data: Data Teams gather and display data from formative assessment results. Through the disaggregation in this step, teams will be able to plan for the acceleration of learning for all students.

2. Analyze data and prioritize needs: Data Teams identify strengths and needs of student performance and then form inferences based on the data. Data Teams also prioritize by focusing on the most urgent needs of the learners.

3. Establish SMART goals: Teams collaboratively set incremental goals. These short-term goals are reviewed and revised throughout the data cycle.

4. Select instructional strategies: Teams collaboratively identify research-based instructional strategies. The determination is based on the analysis in Step 2.

5. Determine results indicators: Data Teams monitor their use of strategies to determine the impact and effectiveness of their efforts. This step allows Data Teams to make mid-course corrections.

6. Monitor and evaluate results: Data Teams monitor and reflect on their progress. Teams shift their focus depending on whether goals are or are not met.

The Data Teams Lens

This book has been separated into different sections to allow you to see Data Teams through the many different lenses (*see* Exhibit I.2). Whether you are an administrator, teacher, instructional coach, specialist, or one of the numerous other positions that can exist within education, Data Teams is a process that you can shape to meet your needs, roles, and responsibilities.

The primary purpose of a Data Team is to improve student learning. Data Teams improve student learning by improving teaching and leadership. In the first section of this book, the authors will capture the pivotal roles of standards, formative assessment, literacy, and instruction in the Data Teams process.

The Data Teams structure is designed so that acceleration and intervention

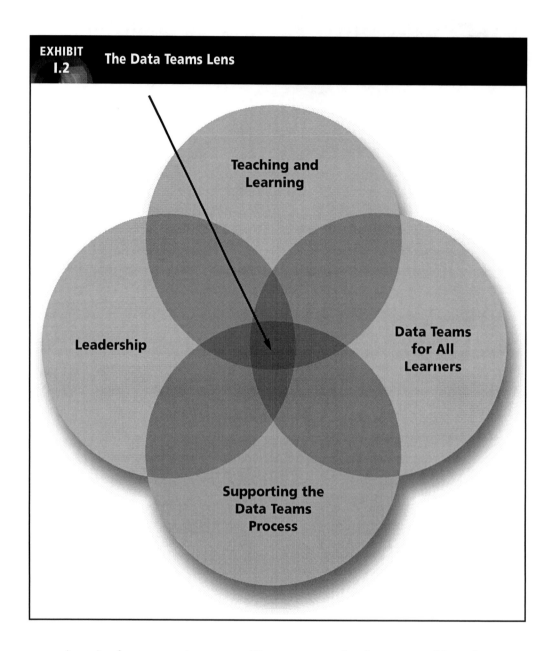

EXHIBIT I.2   The Data Teams Lens

occur in a timely, systematic manner. The process makes learners and learning visible. When teams have this level of transparency, it's empowering to know that they will collaboratively strive to meet the needs of all learners through systematic, targeted, timely intervention. Data Teams are not only designed to help the "bubble kids" reach proficiency; Data Teams are designed to ensure that all students are learning and making progress toward reaching proficiency levels.

Behind every successful Data Team is a successful Data Team leader. That leader may come in the form of a teacher, a parent, a principal, a superintendent, or a school system. Effective leadership is needed to launch any important school initiative, but Data Teams need strong school-based leadership to provide guidance, direction, vision, support, and feedback during the Data Teams journey.

Data Teams are the most powerful professional development that we have experienced. This type of professional development needs to be nurtured, massaged, monitored, and coached. We need to devote the same kind of care and attention to Data Teams as we would to our prized garden, vintage automobile, or top 40 record collection.

Data Teams: The Big Picture will help you see the multiple lenses needed before you embark on your Data Teams journey.

Data Teams are a model for continuous, collaborative action that inspires and empowers professionals to improve teaching, learning, and leadership for all.

DATA TEAMS TRAINING MANUAL, THIRD EDITION, 2010

References

Reeves, D.B. 2010. *Data Teams*, third edition. Englewood, CO: Lead + Learn Press.

SECTION 1

Teaching and Learning

Standards and Assessment in the Data Teams Process

A PRACTICAL LENS

> *"In a classroom where formative assessment is in full flower, you'll find both teachers and students monitoring the success of their efforts by using an assessment-based estimate to determine how much learning has taken place."*
>
> POPHAM, 2009*

Dr. Brandon Doubek shows us the role of standards and assessments in the Data Teams process. He shows us an explicit process used to determine priority teaching and learning targets that Data Teams use as roadmaps on their journey. Formative assessment is at the heart of what we do as educators. Dr. Doubek also increases our understanding of assessment literacy and illustrates the assessment options that Data Teams may use to measure the impact of teaching and learning.

Dr. Doubek outlines a specific research-based process that educators use to determine the "standards that matter most" for student success. **How will your Data Teams embrace and use the process to determine your roadmap?** Dr. Doubek also outlines several assessment options for educators. **How might these options impact your selection of an assessment method?**

*Popham, J. 2009. *Unlearned Lessons: Six Stumbling Blocks to Our Schools' Success.* Cambridge, MA: Harvard Education Press, p. 35.

CHAPTER 1

Standards and Assessment in the Data Teams Process

BRANDON DOUBEK, Ed.D.

If only medical thermometers could tell us how much
and to what extend students have internalized learning
experiences, teachers' lives would be much easier.

Most of my friends in the field of education enjoy communicating their ideas about the educational process in some way. We speak about what we teach, how we teach it, and whether or not students are "getting it." It is a social process, as well as a feedback process. The Data Teams process provides a similar medium although it is more structured with a focus on data from several forms of assessments. These data are derived from assessments that permit teachers and students to discover the extent to which instruction on specific, prioritized curriculum standards has made an impact on student learning. Beyond the advantageous nature of peer collaboration, the Data Teams process reflects the interdependent features of student learning through a close examination of curriculum, instruction, and assessment. However, the reliance upon data to "drive" instruction requires an examination of the "bookends" of learning, curriculum, and assessment in order to understand this influence on the instructional process.

Measuring Prioritized, Power Standards in the Data Teams Process

Because curriculum is the "what" that is measured by assessments and analyzed in Data Teams, it is critical that prioritized, or Power Standards, meet three criteria to determine their place in the hierarchy of what students need to know and be able to do. These three criteria are *endurance, leverage,* and *readiness* (Ainsworth, 2003).

It is only through a close justification process of each standard using all three criteria, rather than just one or two, that gives each individual skill, process, and concept its true "power."

Endurance

The first criterion is *endurance,* or those enduring understandings that will have longevity in a lifetime of learning. These may include, but are not limited to, the ability to read nonfiction text, to add whole numbers, to understand cause and effect, or to classify information by comparing and contrasting. Endurance should justify the "so what" factor of teaching and learning, or what students contend as, "Why do I need to know this?" In using images of famous portraits like the Mona Lisa or reading medicine labels, educators may draw analogies to the ways in which the ability to know or do something relevant, like read nonfiction text, is a skill that lasts for a lifetime, or has knowledge "fame" unto itself.

Furthermore, in justifying a standard based on endurance, teachers may derive "hooks" for the instructional process based on real life applications inherent in the enduring understandings of curriculum standards. For example, if I am teaching the concept of resistance in a science class, I may begin by asking my class about things in life they resist and what occurs as a result of that resistance; this grounds the instruction in something relevant to students. In the Data Teams process, this curricular conversation may be discussed as members are finding strengths and obstacles in Step 2 or in Step 4 as they discuss possible engagement strategies. In this light, curriculum is interdependent with the instructional process just as it is intertwined with assessment procedures.

Leverage

The second criterion for prioritizing a standard is *leverage,* or the horizontal alignment to those specific skills, processes, and concepts in other content areas, including music, art, and physical education, in addition to the top four core areas that are usually tested on state measures of achievement. In the justification process for prioritization, a certain level of specificity is required. Making a connection to an explicit skill in a specific content area requires knowledge of other content standards. In this way, Data Teams that consist of different content areas, rather than the typical content-focused, homogenous grouping of teachers, may add an additional layer of interdisciplinary thought to the Data Teams process. This type of configuration may also lend itself to project-based performance assessments both in classroom-based practices for comprehensive schools and in community projects for schools seeking alternative, authentic, twenty-first century learning experiences. Moreover, this type of shared assessment process may also allow for greater inter-rater reliability when two or more teachers create learning opportunities that require sharing a rubric for interdisciplinary experiences for students. In this way Data Teams may be used to find connections to multiple content areas rather than compartmentalizing content area domain knowledge.

Readiness

The third and final criterion for prioritizing standards is *readiness*, or those particular skills that are prerequisites for future skills. This vertical alignment of content skills prepares learners for new understandings that they will encounter later in a course of study or in future courses, or most importantly, in future life applications. It is a system of building blocks. For instance, the ability to count from one to ten is a prerequisite for counting from one to one hundred, which is a prerequisite for adding two-digit numbers, which is a prerequisite for solving word problems containing two-digit numbers. As they explore assessment data, teachers, through the Data Teams process, examine and sequence learning experiences from prioritized standards based on prerequisite knowledge and understandings that students must acquire. As these discrete aspects of retention are measured through concrete assessments, teachers must adjust instruction based on the results of students' levels of knowing prerequisite skills and concepts, as well as students' abilities to retain new information from curriculum standards.

Challenges of Curriculum Mapping

Students Who Have Not Mastered the Required Skills

So often this facet of the teaching process, usually in the form of curriculum mapping, can be problematic for teachers who face unique challenges with students who have not yet mastered the required skill level or have not followed Bloom's cognitive taxonomy levels (Bloom, 1985), which range from knowledge/remembering (Level 1) to synthesis/creating (Level 6) of certain skills within prioritized standards (see Exhibit 1.1).

Time Requirements. Teachers often complain that, after creating a time line for prioritized standards to be taught, there is still not enough time to ensure that all students reach the required level of mastery. While some students may only reach Level 2 of Bloom's taxonomy (understanding), the standard may necessitate the

EXHIBIT 1.1	Bloom's Cognitive Taxonomy
Level 1 **Remembering**	Being able to recall facts; denotation
Level 2 **Understanding**	Being able to summarize or paraphrase in your own words
Level 3 **Applying**	Being able to use information in a new context
Level 4 **Analyzing**	Being able to compare, contrast, sequence, classify, or otherwise break down information into its component parts
Level 5 **Evaluating**	Being able to justify reasons for the use of information
Level 6 **Creating**	Being able to create something new or put something back together in a new way

mastery of Level 4 (analyzing). This conundrum requires a reevaluation of the prioritized standards to confirm that all identified "safety net" (Reeves, 1996) Power Standards can indeed be justified by all three criteria. Moreover, the Data Teams process provides an opportunity for teachers to collaboratively engage in discussion around instructional strategies that may provide additional solutions for students who struggle, or for those students who, after receiving mediation through additional instructional methodologies, do not show increased progress toward the (Bloom) level of understanding in the standard.

Balanced Assessment Practices. Teachers must also reflect upon their assessment practices to verify that assessment procedures are balanced so that students have the opportunity to demonstrate mastery through more question types than selected-response questions (multiple choice, true/false, matching, etc.). Unfortunately, these are often the sole method of computer-generated and teacher-edition series assessments. This balance in assessment systems requires more than quantitative assessments can measure; it entails creating assessment questions that consist of constructed, qualitative responses or that involve performance assessments.

Response to Interventions. Finally, teachers must consider the use of response to interventions when both instruction and assessment procedures fail to increase student growth. Response to intervention allows students who would otherwise become part of the over-identification process for special education to become successful through other modes of instruction. Each of these reevaluation procedures should be considered after teachers analyze data for strengths and obstacles in Step 2 of the Data Teams process and as they recommend instructional strategies in penultimate Step 4.

As teachers find the strengths of proficient students, they should list as many pieces of evidence from student work as possible. These strengths often show what proficient students can do that nonproficient students cannot, and they can be used to select strategies that will foster change based on the obstacles of nonproficient students. Likewise, the Data Teams process has the potential to allow members to reflect on their practice by "borrowing" strengths of practice from other colleagues in the process of cross-pollinating instructional ideas. By creating meaningful results indicators in Step 5, members reveal not only expectations for students, but adult expectations for performance.

Differences in Content Area Standards

A second problem often identified in prioritizing standards for use in Data Teams is the unique differences in content area standards. While mathematics standards are inherently linear with algebraic building blocks tacit in each course of study, courses in the language arts usually contain prioritized standards that are ongoing and last throughout a year of study. For example, students are always building vocabulary in every content area course, but while this skill may be prioritized only once in a curricular scope and sequence of a school year, it does not disappear. By allowing students to become metacognitive about the information they are internalizing and explicitly teaching students how to retain vocabulary through various instructional strategies, teachers are creating autonomous learners through a gradual release of responsibility for the onus of teaching and learning from the teacher to the student. Thus, the prioritized standard of vocabulary acquisition in the language arts, if it is given due diligence through the middle school years and demonstrated through various forms of assessment (as evidenced in the Data Teams collaborative process), might not become a prioritized standard in the high school years. Because reading comprehension is cumulative and because text levels vary by each year of academic study in all content areas, Power Standards are generally identified and measured each year throughout the K–12 continuum, as is the case with writing standards. However, if teachers are making the best use of the Data Teams process by using both pre- and post-test assessments, each Power Standard measured and discussed in Data Teams should extend the levels of readiness as prerequisites for higher levels of understanding and retention. Additionally, the use of pre-tests may also be used to differentiate instruction not only by ability, but by readiness, learning style, or interest as extensions of Step 4 in the Data Teams process.

The Purpose of Assessments in Data Teams

Almost anyone can copy or create an assessment that will quantify levels of knowledge, but the conscientious, intentional assessment creator will measure the extent to which students have internalized new and prerequisite learning based on the amount of time spent on instruction and the importance of a Power Standard. Just as the dashboard of any transportation vehicle tells us our levels of fuel, purposeful assessments should inform both students and teachers of the extent to which a learner has reached some level of mastery for each prioritized standard. Although our dashboards are easy to read and require little thinking for the consequent action of adding more gas, oil, or water to our vehicles, assessments are more complex and require us to make inferences and generalizations about our learners. Because this is such a complex process and requires time, it is understandable that many teachers would rather copy text series questions or use all quantitative questions that are most easily graded. If only medical thermometers could tell us how much and to what extent students have internalized learning experiences, teachers' lives would be much easier. However, until technology reaches that capability, our assessments must be carefully constructed to accurately reflect students' retention of learning experiences after they have occurred. In this regard, most assessments are ex post facto; thus, the amount of time that elapses after assessments have been given after learning is what usually distinguishes them as either formative or summative assessments.

Since educators collect various forms of data to use in Data Teams meetings, those data should be valid and reliable measurements of students' understandings. Moreover, data from assessments that are most useful will reveal changes that should be made in the instructional process in the form of midcourse revisions of instructional strategy choices. In addition, standards can be revisited to make certain they can be justified by all three prioritization criteria.

Validity of Assessment Instruments

While many educational research texts (Cohen, 2007; Frankel and Wallen, 2003; Gall, Borg, and Gall, 1996) mention various forms of validity (e.g., content validity, construct validity, criterion-related validity, etc.), for the purposes of this chapter related to the Data Teams process, the most expeditious way for teachers to validate assessment instruments would seem to be to:

1. Make sure that each item truly measures the prioritized standard

2. Examine the Bloom's cognitive taxonomy level of each question item associated with each prioritized standard

3. Check the number of items based on the time spent on instruction (i.e., if 25 percent of instruction was spent on fractions, then 25 percent of the assessment items should measure fractions)

4. Ask a colleague to assess whether the instrument measures the first three criteria.

In the use of formative assessments, teachers may want to create one question per scaffolded level of Bloom's taxonomy represented by the verbs in the standard. For example, if a standard requires students to analyze, which is Level 4 of Bloom's cognitive taxonomy, a teacher may want to create four questions, one at each level to find out the extent to which students are approaching mastery.

Reliability of Assessment Instruments

Another consideration is the reliability of an assessment. Reliability refers to the extent to which an assessment is consistent, or will yield relatively the same results when it is given repeatedly. While many educational research texts (Cohen, 2007; Frankel and Wallen, 2003; Gall, Borg, and Gall, 1996) mention various forms of reliability (e.g., test–retest, alternative forms, split halves, and internal consistency), for the intentions of this chapter associated with the Data Teams process, the most expeditious way for teachers to determine the reliability of an assessment instrument would be to examine the results, or class averages, of assessments given to more than one group of students of similar proficiency levels. When those averages are close from one class to the next, the reliability is high. When those averages show large differences, the reliability would be in question.

This process is easiest for secondary teachers who teach more than one section of a course or for elementary teachers who can compare with other teachers on the same grade level. For those in smaller elementary or secondary schools, it may be necessary to compare assessments over a period of several years or to find those common measures from one grade level to another with other local instructors. However, with modern Internet technology, teachers may be able to co-create assessments with colleagues who have similar students and compare them with educators in other like places.

Most importantly, assessments should give students and teachers the most immediate feedback possible as a check for understanding. Learners can only change their thinking when they receive feedback in some form, and the more timely the feedback is, the more quickly a possible change can occur.

Importance of Feedback

In the same way that students receive feedback from teachers, the Data Teams process allows teachers to receive feedback from their colleagues. When we allow ourselves as educators the experience of looking at data from assessments in an objective manner, rather than becoming emotional over student obstacles as a reflection on the quality of our teaching, data can become our guiding beacons for strengths to celebrate and obstacles to overcome. Thus, it is important to examine various levels of data that create opportunities to change instruction and revise curriculum so that we may transcend barriers of academic achievement.

Balancing Assessment Items for Use in Data Teams

Although most state-level assessment data are quantitative in nature, they are not always the most accurate measures of teaching and learning; however, they are used the most because grading is much faster and more concrete. In this age of high-stakes tests that often dictate policy and practice, we must remember that, in our classrooms, we are still the designers, deliverers, and assessors of learning experiences. We must determine the individual needs of our students by assessing their strengths and challenges in pre-tests and by assessing their growth in post-test measures. In doing so, and by using the Data Teams process to collect feedback and logical objectivity from our colleagues, we stand to increase the probability of students becoming more confident when they are faced with high-stakes challenges. For this reason, we should examine the types of possible data for use on assessments in Data Teams for the purpose of scaffolding test-taking procedures to demystify some of the processes of assessment.

Although educational research on assessment instrumentation alludes to four main types of data (nominal, ordinal, interval, and ratio levels), for the purpose of this chapter, we will explore types of assessment data responses that reveal purposeful information relevant to the most commonly used assessments. Because quantitative data, or data that can be counted, are used most, we will begin here.

Quantitative Data

Selected-response questions on assessments yield binary results (two possible choices) for true/false–type questions, while multiple-choice and matching questions, plus fill-in-the-blank questions with word banks, may utilize tertiary (three) or greater possible responses. Because high-stakes tests make the greatest use of multiple-choice formats for faster grading practices, educators may experiment on formative assessments with scaffolding only two choices, then three, and so on, up to the point at which the potential assessment utilizes the greatest number of possible responses (usually four or five). This is particularly useful for building confidence in special-education learners and English language learners, but it is also helpful for general education students and advanced students on AP, IB, SAT, and ACT tests. In the Data Teams process, an analysis of these results may yield a greater understanding for revising instruction and assessment methodology. As mentioned, however, quantitative data are not the "be-all" and "end-all" of assessment; too often these selected-response, objective types of questions are used in isolation just because high-stakes tests utilize them the most.

Qualitative Data

Educators must take into account the fact that not all students test well on selected-response items and that better assessments are balanced in terms of selected- and constructed-response-type questions. If the purpose of assessment is to provide feedback and to guide instruction, then qualitative (constructed and extended constructed) responses, or those responses most commonly known as subjective (essay or short-answer), must be used to gather "data-rich" information. Students may be able to play the quintessential "guessing game" on selected-response items, but in the collection of qualitative data, students are usually required to, at the very least, explain something in their own words (Bloom's Level 2: understanding). Most often these data provide interwoven ideas, connections, and personal relationships that require them to use or apply information (Level 3), analyze through comparison, classification, or sequencing (Level 4), justify (Level 5), or create something new from what they have gleaned from all scaffolded information (Level 6).

Just because these assessments take longer to grade or students are not tested in this format on high-stakes tests, or because rubrics may take longer to create, there is no excuse to exclude them from the assessment process. Because we are trying to make accurate inferences—inferences that change student thinking and guide instructional practice—we must make every attempt to gather the most efficient data that allow for immediate, timely feedback for students and teachers. In this way we may create more valid assessments with colleagues who may be able to help us in this endeavor. Data Teams allow teachers to collaboratively create and score assessments, and they also allow teachers to discuss categorical strengths of students when rubrics and checklists are used. The potential discussions that qualitative data yield provide teachers the opportunity to reveal the layers of thinking behind not just what students know, but why and how they know it. This type of thinking cannot be revealed so easily in quantitative questioning.

The Relationship Between Assessment and Literacy

We may draw parallels between assessment and Eliot Eisner's definition of literacy (Eisner, 1994). According to Eisner, literacy is the ability to construct, create, and communicate (all Bloom, Level 6) meaning in a variety of representational forms. Text is referred to essentially as anything that can be sensed; therefore, students might use any of their senses to process printed words, music symbols or sounds, art, dance, chemistry, baking, football, or theater. When students are constructing meaning by using their senses (sight, sound, touch, smell, and taste) to receive information (Bloom, 1985), meaning is then created as it is perceived by the brain based on prior knowledge and experiences. This created meaning must be expressed in some form as it is communicated publicly or in private. This last phase of the literacy cycle may be evidenced in assessment, or the communication of meaning in some representational form. Hence, if we are only providing answers for students to choose from in the assessment process via selected-response items, what happens if the items that we attempt to measure, or generate for students to select from, are not among the items that students would choose? Only through the balance of constructed- and selected-response items can we begin to create opportunities for more students' success. Although subjective responses may not be as clearly identified in the assessment process, the use of rubrics and checklists attempts to objectify the subjective. Further-more, this relationship between assessment and literacy may also allow teachers to more deeply explain strengths and obstacles in Step 2 of the Data Teams process. While the balance of selected- and constructed-response items on assessments is a critical component of gathering useful data, we must also explore the relationship and use of formative and summative assessments as they are used in Data Teams.

Balancing Assessment Systems "Hand to Glove" in Data Teams

If schools are creating truly balanced assessment systems, they will be thinking with the end in mind—that end usually being some high-stakes test or a comprehensive end-of-course examination. Building backwards, each summative assessment should contain the same level of rigor, as indicated by curriculum standards. Then, formative assessments leading to each summative assessment should be scaffolded to include items that allow teachers and students to know how prepared they are for eventual summative assessments. While the Data Teams process most often uses assessment data from common formative assessments (Ainsworth, 2006), summative assessments might also be used if they allow students and teachers to make midcourse corrections that will benefit the learning process.

Because different levels of assessment are often in question in terms of their use in Data Teams and in classroom practice, these levels should be clarified so that their use contributes to a common language for educators and students. In my work in districts throughout the United States and Canada, educators often question which data are most useful in the Data Teams process. The answer to this question should always point to the purpose of the assessment. That purpose should be clear not only to educators but to students as well. But we also must classify each assessment level so that each level aligns "hand to glove." This will help students to feel confident and will help them to persist in allowing us to measure their understandings.

Formative Assessments

Formative assessments are generally comprised of two main categories:

- Level 1: Simple or informal, which require no paper and pencil
- Level 2: Complex or formal, which do require paper and pencil

Level 1 tends to be composed of observation, questions asked in class, or anything that allows teachers to check for understanding so that students receive immediate feedback without writing. However, Level 1 assessments are less concrete than Level 2 (formal formative) assessments. Level 2 assessments are more concerned with short, written responses that are easy to assess and that also give teachers and students feedback. However, more often than not, this feedback does not occur as quickly as it does in Level 1 assessments. Common formative assessments (Ainsworth, 2003) fall into the Level 2 category, and because data are concrete, they allow teachers to adjust instruction with feedback from their colleagues, whereas Level 1 assessments are so immediate that input from colleagues is not necessarily warranted.

Formative assessments have the most profound impact on student achievement because they are nonthreatening, are not used for grading procedures, and allow students to grow and practice for summative assessments. In the Data Teams process, teachers create action plans in Step 3 by creating SMART goals, using the results of these short-cycle assessments to move students who have not mastered a curriculum standard in a positive direction. Moreover, teachers in heterogeneous groupings by content area or grade level may discover possibilities of moving students into flexible groups that allow for greater differentiation to meet the needs of diverse learners as teachers chart and graph data in Step 1 of the Data Teams process.

Summative Assessments

If these formative assessments are aligned in terms of format and rigor, then summative assessments should reflect the growth of this process.

Like formative assessments, summative assessments fall into two categories:

- Level 3: Simple or informal summative assessments
- Level 4: Complex or formal summative assessments

Level 3 assessments are based on shorter pieces of new information, like chapter or even some unit assessments, vocabulary building, or the metacognition of study skills associated with content area learning. These assessments are used for grades, but feedback may not be as immediate as in formative assessments because Level 3 assessments usually take longer to grade. It is also more likely for Level 3 summative assessments to be used in Data Teams because there is still an opportunity for students to grow from the feedback from this assessment. When teachers are using "mastery" models of grading, and students are allowed to rewrite essays or short tests that fall into this category, Data Teams conversations can be quite rich about the growth that students make as they journey toward deep understandings of their current study. Furthermore, when these shorter summative assessments are aligned to more comprehensive assessments, they should poten-tially show high levels of predictive validity for more high-stakes types of tests.

Level 4 summative assessments are more complex and formal, and they often represent a sense of finality in the learning process for grade levels or entire courses of study. High-stakes tests fall into this category. These types of assessments are most often comprehensive in nature, and the time that students and teachers wait to receive feedback is considerably longer. While some larger unit tests, performance assessments, or research projects may be useful for the Data Teams process, most often these assessments are cumulative grading mechanisms or high-stakes tests for which students and teachers only see results numbers without being able to examine individual responses to specific questions. In the case of these final assessments, the use of these data in Data Teams is often pointless, because teachers and students may not be paired in the same setting after the results are delivered. Even with some end-of-course assessments and final exams, unless students are allowed to view their responses, there is no chance of growth from the assessment itself.

Performance Assessments in Data Teams

The use of performance-based assessments, or projects that require multiple modalities of learning and multiple intelligences (Gardner, 1983), are equally valuable for discussions in Data Teams. Because multiple criteria for assessments (e.g., presentation delivery, artistry, organization, group process, etc.) are potential categories for measurement and provide valid and reliable data when rubrics are constructed in advance and often with student input, these criteria can also be analyzed both formatively and summatively in Data Teams discussions. Because students are required to create products that may be differentiated, and because performance assessments are much closer to the expectations of the work world, the potential for analyzing strengths and obstacles in Step 2 should yield superior outcomes and exemplars upon which students may build. Although most Data Teams that are observed by The Leadership and Learning Center focus on the use of common formative assessments in grade-level or content area groupings, it would not be beyond the realm of possibility for groups of piano teachers, football coaches, or classroom teachers using performances or portfolios to engage in the beneficial protocol that is the Data Teams process. In the same way that writing teachers often use rubrics to assess content and organization of student writing samples, performance samples may yield similar data for educators to analyze in Data Teams. The use of data from portfolios, or from student work samples (reading, writing, journals, etc.) gathered over a period of time, may also provide another viable alternative for data collection. These data may also be analyzed in Data Teams.

Helpful Reminders for Data Teams

Whether we are graphing data from common formative assessments, summative assessments, leadership data (e.g., walk-throughs, attendance, etc.), or performance data for use by Data Teams, the data must be useful and something that we have prioritized for improvement. Also, in the same way that there must be a clear purpose for why we choose to measure something on an assessment—assessments from which we should be able to make inferences—data must be visually represented so that the viewer gains a rapid perspective of the various levels of proficiency. It is often helpful in charts and graphs to show the percentage(s) or lines of demarcation that separate these various levels, because the scales for

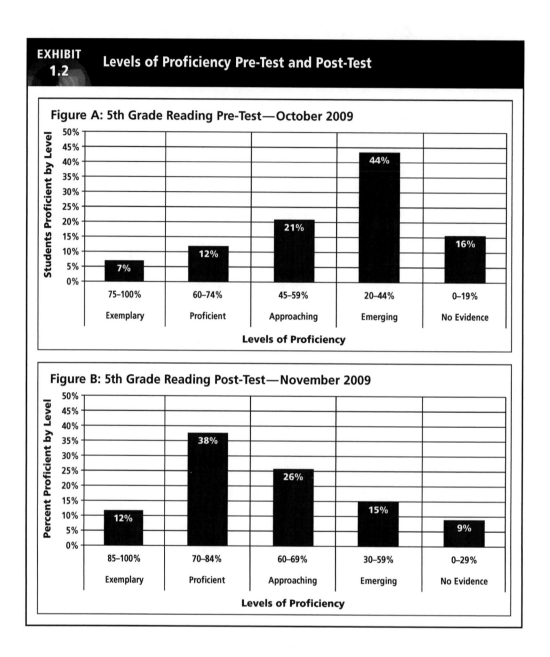

EXHIBIT 1.2   Levels of Proficiency Pre-Test and Post-Test

Figure A: 5th Grade Reading Pre-Test—October 2009

Students Proficient by Level

| 75–100% Exemplary | 60–74% Proficient | 45–59% Approaching | 20–44% Emerging | 0–19% No Evidence |
| 7% | 12% | 21% | 44% | 16% |

Levels of Proficiency

Figure B: 5th Grade Reading Post-Test—November 2009

Percent Proficient by Level

| 85–100% Exemplary | 70–84% Proficient | 60–69% Approaching | 30–59% Emerging | 0–29% No Evidence |
| 12% | 38% | 26% | 15% | 9% |

Levels of Proficiency

proficiency may vary from a pre-test to a post-test or from one Power Standard to another. As is the case in Exhibit 1.2, it is important to make sure that we are comparing two apples or two oranges. If this is not the case, the justification should be noted for a reader. Notice that in Exhibit 1.2, from Figure A to Figure B, the first scale level of "exemplary" changes by 10 percent.

It is also important that, if we are measuring several aspects (sometimes called "strands" or component parts) within a prioritized standard, we have some way of knowing which items of an assessment measure those parts. For example, if we are measuring a Power Standard on reading comprehension that contains both inferences and generalizations, we are able to track those items for mention in Step 2 of analyzing strengths and obstacles. See the example in Exhibit 1.3.

EXHIBIT 1.3	Power Standard Assessment Itemization	
Parts of the Power Standard	**Item Numbers**
Inferences	1, 4, 6
Generalizations	2, 3, 7

In all Data Teams training sessions, it is usually explained that in Step 1, students are placed in groups (e.g., proficient, already close, far to go, and in need of extra support), based on data already charted. In Step 2, the goal is to move those who are approaching proficiency into the proficient category by analyzing their strengths and obstacles. Then, in Step 3, a SMART goal is set for students who are approaching proficiency. This does not mean that we do not set goals for the other two groups of students. In fact, we should analyze each group's strengths and weaknesses, then set another SMART goal for each other group and choose unique strategies in Step 4 that will help that particular group. Ultimately, we then set results indicators in Step 5 for each group. Each set of students should have a goal and a plan of action, as well as results indicators that show the adult behaviors via the strategies chosen to make sure that each group moves forward by at least one level of proficiency.

Grading and the Data Teams Process for Educational Leaders

Although grading remains a contentious issue in 2010, it is not beyond educational leaders to analyze marking practices as another process in collecting school, department, or grade-level data. In fact, I have had conversations with leaders in different states and provinces who have collected such data and use them each quarter or semester in the Data Teams process as a method for analyzing grading practices. In the same way that teachers use formative and summative data in Data Teams, leaders may chart these data in Step 1, find the strengths and obstacles in

Step 2, then use Step 3 to set SMART goals. Because instructional strategies are not applicable to this process, educational leaders often begin public and private conversations with faculty and support staff to create schoolwide grading policies as their Step 4 in the Data Teams process. For Step 5, educational leaders propose leadership supports (cause data) that will positively impact teaching and learning. In this way, Data Teams may involve all aspects of the educational process, from curriculum and assessments that impact instruction to leadership that supports all learning. Through these avenues, the goal is to move all students in a positive direction.

References

Ainsworth, L. 2003. *Power Standards.* Englewood, CO: Lead + Learn Press.

———. 2006. *Common Formative Assessments.* Thousand Oaks, CA: Corwin.

Bloom, B.S., ed. 1985. *Developing Talent in Young People.* New York, NY: Ballantine Books.

Cohen, J. 2007. *Research Methods in Education,* 6th ed. New York, NY: Routledge.

Eisner, E. 1994. *Cognition and Curriculum.* New York: Teachers College Press.

Frankel, J., and N. Wallen. *Educational Research: A Guide to the Process,* 2nd ed. Mahwah, NJ: Erlbahm.

Gall, M.D., W.R. Borg, and J.P. Gall. 1996. *Educational Research: An Introduction,* 6th ed. White Plains, NY: Longman.

Gardner, H. 1983. *Frames of the Mind: The Theory of Multiple Intelligences.* New York, NY: Basic Books.

Reeves, D.B. 1996. *Making Standards Work.* Englewood, CO: Lead + Learn Press.

Data Teams: Improving Literacy Instruction for All Students

A PRACTICAL LENS

"Generous amounts of close, purposeful reading, rereading, writing, and talking, as under-emphasized as they are in K–12 education, are the essence of authentic literacy. These simple activities are the foundation for a trained, powerful mind—and a promising future."

MIKE SCHMOKER, 2006*

Dr. Angela Peery shows us that Data Teams that embrace literacy as a team focus make incredible strides in improving teaching and learning. She helps us to see the vital role of literacy in preparing our students for tomorrow's future.

Examine your standards. **Where are students asked to demonstrate their thinking through communication? How are students asked to process the information they are learning? Just like many other schools have already done, how can your Data Teams use literacy to help prepare our students for the future?**

*Schmoker, M. 2006. *Results Now: How We Can Achieve Unprecedented Improvements in Teaching and Learning.* Alexandria, VA: ASCD, p. 53.

CHAPTER 2

Data Teams: Improving Literacy Instruction for All Students

ANGELA B. PEERY, ED.D.

Tightening the focus on key literacy skills—from the superintendent and central administration levels, down to each building, to each classroom, down to the progress for each individual student, as monitored both by individual teachers and by Data Teams—helps schools achieve unparalleled gains.

Getting Data Teams Up and Running: A Vignette

Elkhart, Indiana, is a typical midwestern city in many respects, but it is also a unique community. This city of approximately 52,000 residents in northern Indiana is a two-hour drive from Chicago and is only fifteen miles from legendary South Bend, the home of Notre Dame University. Elkhart's main employers are the musical instrument and recreational vehicle industries, along with other light-manufacturing companies. The downturn in the economy in 2009 and 2010 hit Elkhart particularly hard, with the unemployment rate spiking as high as 18 percent in some media reports and generating multiple visits by candidate (and later President) Barack Obama.

Elkhart Community Schools consist of twenty-one buildings and just fewer than 1,900 employees. The system enrolls more than 13,000 students, 53 percent of whom are white, 16 percent of whom are black, and 23 percent of whom are Hispanic. More than 3,000 students have a native language other than English. In order to increase student achievement, the school system conducted basic training in the Data Teams model for all teachers over a period of three years and then began full implementation in the 2008–2009 school year.

In 2007, after several years of unsatisfactory performance, Roosevelt Primary School was reconstituted (along with one other Elkhart elementary school) by the state of Indiana. Roosevelt began the Data Teams process in earnest the following fall in order to improve instruction for all students. Roosevelt's principal at the time, Beth Bouchard, was concerned about improving literacy instruction for all students but was also focused on the high number of second-language learners. Each grade level became an intact Data Teams. Additionally, there were Data Teams for the special subjects (music, physical education, and art), English as a Second Language (ESL), and special education. All Data Teams met during extended collaboration times at least once weekly and focused on skills they selected, which were related to the Elkhart Community Schools Power Standards.

In that first year, results were inconsistent, as teams strived to comprehend their standards better and to work more collaboratively than ever before, all the while being monitored closely by the state. However, there were some noticeable successes, and a focus on literacy schoolwide was sustained. In less than one month of instruction, kindergarten students proficient in identifying all capital and lowercase letters of the alphabet grew from 64 percent to 81 percent (personal communication, Beth Bouchard, February 2010). The teachers had been working with students on this skill for several Data Teams cycles but had employed a new instructional strategy—classification—in this particular cycle to get the dramatic results. The school's cross-curricular focus on literacy was perhaps best exemplified by the physical education team, who had a word wall in the gym. They constantly used the words in instruction and monitored the number of words that students knew. They saw increases throughout the year, especially with their ESL students (personal communication, Beth Bouchard, February 2010).

Roosevelt experienced moderate success in the spring of 2008, as they achieved adequate yearly progress (AYP) in eight of eleven categories, including overall proficiency in English. In comparison, in the spring of 2007, Roosevelt had achieved AYP in only two of eleven categories, none of which were English. One student subgroup's progress was notable: Hispanic students made AYP in 2008 after not reaching that milestone in 2007.

Roosevelt Primary School continues to use Data Teams as part of its school improvement efforts, as do all schools in the Elkhart system. After several years of curriculum design work, accompanied by the use of Data Teams, Elkhart was number one in the group of the twenty largest Indiana school districts in improving their ISTEP+ (state test) results over a three-year period (Hill, J., presentation, August 2009). Dr. John Hill, Director of Curriculum, embraces Data Teams as an improvement strategy:

> Elkhart Community Schools' universal use of consistent and frequent collaboration among teachers with the five-step Data Teams process has enabled our students to grow more quickly than their counterparts in other urban school corporations in Indiana. During the three-year time span from 2006 to 2008, Elkhart students led Indiana's largest school corporations increasing the number of students who passed Indiana's high-stakes assessment (ISTEP+) by more than 2 percent (personal communication, February 2010).

Effective Literacy Instruction: What All Children Need

Children of all ages in America's schools need high-quality literacy instruction so that they can thrive in a twenty-first century, global society that will make unprecedented demands on them as viewers, listeners, readers, speakers, writers, and consumers. Being literate across texts and technologies is so important that many prominent educational researchers emphasize cross-curricular literacy as the core of a student's education (Allington and Cunningham, 2010; Reeves, 2010; Schmoker, 2006).

Decades of information about literacy achievement show the need for American teachers to continue to focus on literacy and to ensure that all student groups, especially those who have been previously marginalized, achieve at high levels. In elementary literacy, National Assessment of Educational Progress (NAEP) data indicate that the achievement gap between non-Caucasian students and their Caucasian peers is narrowing slightly (Haycock, 2010). However, NAEP results still show that 37 percent of America's fourth-graders fail to achieve basic levels of reading proficiency (Lonigan and Shanahan, n.d.). When these results are disaggregated so that one can examine the performance within low-income families, ethnic minority groups, and English language learners, the failure rate is even more dismal (Lonigan and Shanahan, n.d.). Continued attention on literacy for all, with decisive interventions made for those who are underperforming, is necessary in each and every school.

As students get older, their reading achievement unfortunately does not dramatically improve. While Latino students are starting to make small movements toward closing the ethnic achievement gap in NAEP eighth-grade reading, their African-American counterparts are not (Haycock, 2010). Additionally, NAEP reading results for seventeen-year-olds have remained flat for more than twenty years (Haycock, 2010). The reading performance of middle school and high school students has many serious ramifications: Students struggle with textbook reading assignments; limited reading proficiency stalls the learning of critical academic vocabulary; and one of the most commonly cited reasons for dropping out of school is the lack of appropriate literacy skills (Biancarosa and Snow, 2004). If a high school graduate with poor literacy skills enters college, it is highly likely that he or she will need remedial reading and/or writing courses. Historically, college remediation does not bode well for the success of the student; 70 percent of students who take remedial reading courses do not attain a college degree within eight years (Adelman, 2004). In America in 2010 and beyond, a college degree is the basic prerequisite for many careers; therefore, adults without college degrees are limiting their earning power.

In short, children who cannot read well become adults who are not fully prepared to participate in American society. More than 20 percent of American adults read at or below a fifth-grade level (National Institute for Literacy, 2001), a level that is increasingly further and further below the demands of the modern workplace. Literacy is also correlated with poverty. Forty-three percent of people with the lowest literacy skills live in poverty, and 17 percent receive public assistance in the form of food stamps (National Institute for Literacy, 2001). Thus, low-level literacy is very costly in a social and economic sense for all of us. Many of those citizens who lack strong literacy skills become prison inmates. In all age groups surveyed (sixteen to twenty-four, twenty-five to thirty-nine, and forty and older), incarcerated adults had lower average literacy than adults in those same age groups living in households (National Center for Education Statistics, 2007). The skills of being able to read and write well pay dividends for a lifetime, both personally and professionally, and may literally keep people out of prison and off of the public's dime.

The urgency is clear: Effective literacy instruction throughout all levels of schooling is imperative for individuals and for our society at large. Effective literacy instruction, according to educator and researcher Mike Schmoker (2009), includes sufficient quantities of all of the following: purposeful discussion (in pairs, groups, and whole-class seminars); reading (books, authentic documents—not just worksheets); and writing in all subjects, including mathematics, with a focus on persuasive and interpretive writing.

Using Data Teams to Focus on Literacy Needs

Generally, Data Teams begin their work under the umbrella of needs and goals as articulated in a School Improvement Plan (SIP). Educators at Roosevelt Primary

School, profiled earlier in this chapter, began under such an umbrella with the extra weight of school restructuring imposed upon them by the state department of education. Whale Branch Middle School in Beaufort, South Carolina, started in a similar way: After multiple years of low performance, turnaround specialists in English language arts and mathematics were provided to the school by the state department of education, and an additional directive about increasing the use of writing across the curriculum was given by the principal. Tehipite Middle School in Fresno, California, was in "program improvement" status (because of low achievement) and began the work of Data Teams much in the same way as Whale Branch, meeting many of their academic improvement goals after one sustained year of Data Teams work with a writing emphasis. William Harding High School in Bridgeport, Connecticut, also under state sanctions for underperformance and a low graduation rate, began with Data Teams in all subject areas and quickly found that key reading and writing issues impact learning, attendance, test performance, and credit accrual. All of these schools, and many others with which The Center has worked, enhanced literacy instruction through the use of Data Teams.

So how did they do it? First, to reiterate, at these schools and many others around the nation, an SIP containing specific academic goals frames the most urgent instructional needs. Under this SIP umbrella, some principals choose to direct the work of the Data Teams by saying, for example, "Students' reading skills are of the utmost importance, and reading is the area that our test scores and other information point to as needing improvement. Please begin the work by focusing your Data Teams efforts on reading." Many elementary school principals direct the attention of Data Teams to either their reading or math goals, or to both simultaneously. Other principals are less directive, inviting the teams to focus on any learning goal or curricular aim, whether or not it is directly linked to an SIP goal. In middle and high schools, principals are often comfortable letting their Data Teams work from the established curriculum and then, as the teams discover that low achievement in the subject matter may involve the students' limited academic vocabulary, or their below-grade-level reading skills, or their critical thinking skills as evidenced in their writing, these principals encourage (or demand!) that the teams address these underlying, cross-curricular skills. The faculty at Warren Harding High School, for instance, knows not only that the 2009–2010 school year is the first year of full Data Teams implementation, but also that improving the overall literacy skills of students is critical. (One outgrowth of Data Teams work at Harding has been the testing of all sophomores to determine their reading levels so that teachers can better differentiate and accelerate in order for students to have an increased likelihood of passing their classes and of passing the state's high-stakes test, the CAPT.)

Data Teams' Focus at Kindergarten Level

At the kindergarten level, Data Teams often begin by tracking information about letter recognition, handwriting (for example, letter formation, writing one's name), phonics (letter-sound correspondence), and other basic literacy skills. Kindergarten teachers are required to collect and act upon much of this data anyway; the Data Teams' difference is that teachers sit in a collaborative group, and together they determine strategies to increase learning.

Often, kindergarten teams deepen their work and begin studying students' skills of sequencing, predicting, and determining importance. A kindergarten Data Team at Riverview Elementary School in Elkhart, Indiana, when first moving away from monitoring letter-sound correspondence, decided to assess their students on proficiency in following oral directions. Their first assessment showed that about three-quarters of their students were proficient; this was good news, but it didn't mean that the work of the Data Team could stop. The team decided to assess another skill—the correct sequencing of three events in a text read to the students orally. As the teachers worked through the assessment cycle, they found that their students did need further instruction in this area. Between pre- and post-assessments, many more students became proficient in correct sequencing. In another assessment cycle, the number of students proficient in sight words grew 44 percent between the pre- and post-assessments. Obviously, the instructional strategies used in both of these cycles achieved their intended purpose: increasing the specific, targeted literacy skills of those particular kindergartners within a short time frame (less than a month in each instance). What can other kindergarten teams learn from these examples? Choose an important skill to monitor; work together to select the best strategies possible to employ; don't continue assessing something the students have already mastered (but provide assistance to those few who still need it).

Data Teams' Focus in Early Elementary Grades

In first and second grades, Data Teams often focus on basic reading and writing skills, like sequencing events in a story correctly, retelling a story accurately, making valid predictions based on evidence in a story, writing a complete sentence, using capital letters appropriately, using end marks correctly, or spelling high-frequency words correctly. Teams often experience dramatic results in response to the change in their instructional strategies. One second-grade Data Team in the Concord school system (Indiana) had only 16 percent of its students score proficient or higher in reading comprehension on a pre-assessment, but 92 percent scored proficient or higher on the post-assessment (White, 2007). This is but one of many examples of how teachers put their minds together to increase student achievement rapidly through the five-step Data Teams process. This team statistically moved 1.36 students per day from nonproficiency to proficiency or beyond (White, 2007). Studies like this show that students can be moved incrementally toward greater literacy when Data Teams focus squarely on specific skills and work together to achieve success.

In third grade, significant milestones in literacy exist. One is that students should be able to write a coherent, unified, stand-alone paragraph. To achieve this, certain conventions of print must be followed (most notably, that the student knows to indent). There must be a clear topic sentence plus supporting sentences (usually two or more) that provide details related to the topic sentence. In most state standards, mastery of the single paragraph is clearly delineated at the third-grade level. Students expand their repertoire of writing genres even further, with the amount of personal narrative and fictional narrative decreasing and the amount of expository and persuasive writing increasing. A third-grade Data Team in Concord, Indiana, moved from 24 percent of its students in being proficient in writing a paragraph with an effective topic sentence to 64 percent of them demonstrating this critical skill in only nineteen days of instruction (White, 2007). In reading, students in third grade begin to tackle harder and harder content, and skillful reading is required to learn effectively in math, science, social studies, and other subjects. In third grade, students should have also mastered the basics of reading (accurate decoding, structural analysis, context clues). For many teachers, a significant number of third-grade students still need a great deal of explicit instruction in basic reading skills, and Data Teams can monitor the impact of this instruction very well.

Data Teams' Focus in Upper Elementary Grades

In the upper elementary grades, roughly grades four through six (or in some systems, grades four and five), students refine their reading skills and learn to write multi-paragraph compositions of many types, including creative, narrative, persuasive, analytical, and expository. Analytical writing, including literary response, becomes more important in language arts classes and in preparation for high-stakes tests.

Dawn Bardo, a teacher at Riverview Elementary School, sums up how Data Teams can adapt their work to best assist elementary readers:

> Data Teams have helped ... [us] focus in more on the specific skills
> that are necessary for becoming a proficient reader. We have taken
> the large standards and have reduced them into more manageable

chunks of learning. We started out biting off too broad of a topic and have learned that in order to be more effective, we have had to go smaller (personal communication, 2010).

Ocean View Elementary School in Norfolk, Virginia, encompassing grades pre-kindergarten through five, has used the Data Teams process for a number of years. In 2008, the school celebrated the fact that every fifth-grade student was proficient or higher in the state's standards for reading, writing, and science (http://leadandlearn.com/edgov-article). The school's overall proficiency rate in reading is 96 percent (http://leadandlearn.com/edgov-article), a rate that is enviable and that indicates that many students are learning the most important literacy skills they will need to be successful in middle school, high school, and beyond. The data-monitoring process in place at Ocean View since 2001 has virtually eliminated the achievement gaps for non-Caucasian and free- or reduced-lunch-eligible students. As principal Lauren Campsen notes, "Every time you don't intervene with a child, you've closed doors for that child's future" (http://leadandlearn.com/edgov-article). Through Data Teams and an intensive focus on literacy, Ocean View seems to be opening many doors for its students.

Data Teams' Focus in Middle School

In middle school, students face increasingly harder content-area texts and should be required to write essays that demonstrate critical thinking in all of their classes. A meta-analysis (Graham and Perin, 2007) of almost 600 studies on the teaching of writing concluded that writing is essential for adolescents. They further concluded that students without adequate writing skills suffer disadvantages in multiple subjects in school and later, in the job market. Unfortunately, their analysis also found that student writing is inadequate. Based partially on NAEP data from three decades, many students fail to meet grade-level standards in writing, and more than half of all students entering college are not prepared for the kinds of writing they are expected to do there. Additionally, American businesses spend more than $3 billion annually on writing remediation.

The understanding of these facts, along with the low proficiency levels of their own students, has spurred many middle schools into action. Several middle schools that have used Data Teams in combination with a focus on writing across the curriculum have experienced great success.

Tehipite Middle School in Fresno, California (a school with a high number of free- or reduced-lunch-eligible students and also a significant ELL population), doubled the number of students proficient in organization of writing in just two months. At the end of that year, the second year of Data Teams implementation with a companion focus on increased writing, the school also showed great improvement in both language arts and mathematics on the state's standardized tests.

Bartlett Middle School in Savannah, Georgia, under the leadership of principal Drema Jackson in 2008, realized a gain of 21 percent over the previous year in its eighth-grade writing scores on the state's writing test (given annually only in grades 3, 5, 8, and 11). Jackson attributes this growth to a modified Data Teams process that all eighth-grade teachers used to analyze data from a mock writing test and to the strategies that they immediately enacted (personal communication, March 2008). The targeted strategies were enacted for only about a month prior to the test. This short-term, high-impact process was not only gratifying for the eighth-grade team but also served as an impetus for other grade levels in the school to use a similar process.

Lastly, Waterloo Middle School in central New York exemplifies how a cross-curricular focus on written summaries and academic vocabulary helps students be well prepared for standardized tests and, more importantly, for the work they will need to do in high school and beyond. In the spring of 2008, after about a year of requiring students to write summaries frequently in all classes and explicit vocabulary instruction in the most important terms in each class, language arts scores (on state testing) increased by double digits at all three grade levels (6, 7, and 8). Additionally, math, science, and social studies test scores all increased appreciably.

Data Teams' Focus in High School

High school may be the first place where literacy in the various academic disciplines becomes a huge challenge for students and a conundrum for many teachers, especially those who teach outside of the field of English language arts.

After a full year of conducting monthly, schoolwide writing prompts, analyzing the resulting data, and addressing student needs collaboratively, Woodland High School in South Carolina went from academic watch status to an excellent improvement rating. Concurrently, the school's average SAT score rose twenty-two points, and its high school, exit-level exam passing scores for tenth-graders increased from 41 percent to 65 percent. The improvements required the commitment of all staff, and the school continues to have a 90 percent pass rate on its high school, exit-level test.

Patriot High School in Riverside, California, employs Data Teams as an essential part of its ongoing school improvement efforts. Each team has an action plan and revisits the plan every six weeks (http://www.jusd.k12.ca.us/cnt/docs/Phs0708.pdf).

The school enjoys the highest overall Academic Performance Index rating in its district and also has a higher passing rate for the exit-level state test in English language arts than other schools in its district.

The Bristol Public Schools (Connecticut) have been engaged in a data monitoring and curriculum improvement process, in partnership with The Leadership and Learning Center, since 2002. In the 2006–2007 school year, Bristol Public Schools was the only urban public school system in the state of Connecticut in which all schools made AYP (http://www.leadandlearn.com/files/file/white-paper/Bristol-White-Paper.pdf). Bristol's high schools outscored the state average on the Connecticut Academic Performance Test (CAPT) for tenth grades in both reading and writing in 2007 (http://www.leadandlearn.com/files/file/white-paper/Bristol-White-Paper.pdf) and have continued this trend in literacy (http://www.csde.state.ct.us/public/cedar/nclb/dist_school_nclb_results/2007-08/01_99/17_bristol_district.pdf).

Schools at all levels–primary, elementary, middle, and high–have adapted the Data Teams process so that it works best for their sites, and many schools have chosen to explicitly focus on literacy improvement.

Maximizing the Impact of Data Teams on Literacy in a School and a System

Using the Power Standards

Many systems that have realized success in increasing the literacy skills of their students and closing various achievement gaps (including Bristol, Connecticut; Wayne Township, Indiana; and Norfolk, Virginia) have had, for a number of years, streamlined, clearly communicated curriculum documents based on Power Standards (Ainsworth, 2003)—a prioritized set of essential learnings. Along with system and school site goals expressed in the requisite plans, Power Standards in reading and language arts make clear to students, teachers, parents, and the wider community the specific literacy skills that students must gain at each grade level. When systems use these Power Standards to plan curriculum and assessment, and when student proficiency in these Power Standards is monitored by Data Teams, achievement rises. Tightening the focus on key literacy skills—from the superintendent and central administration level, down to each building, to each classroom, down to the progress for each individual student, as monitored both by individual teachers and by Data Teams—helps schools achieve unparalleled gains.

Using Common Writing Rubrics and Publishing

In addition to basing grade-level curricula and assessment on identified Power Standards, systems can also articulate some of their essential literacy learnings through publication and use of common writing rubrics. Elkhart Community Schools (Indiana) recently had a literacy task force made up of classroom teachers and instructional coaches that developed a writing handbook to help guide instruction in all of its schools. This handbook includes an analytic writing rubric for each grade, grades kindergarten through six, and additional rubrics for middle school and high school. Each rubric is accompanied by writing samples and commentary that explains the score so that teachers can use the samples to guide instruction for their own students. Several schools in the system are using the new rubrics (or shortened forms of them) to monitor students' writing proficiency in a Data Teams process so that students are well prepared for their state writing tests— and, of course, so that teachers can provide ongoing, formative feedback to students so that students can continuously improve their writing and reach or surpass grade-level expectations. At Mary Beck Elementary School in Elkhart, Chief Academic Officer Jeff Komins has been pleased with the steady improvements that students have shown in their writing over a the course of the school year on practice writing prompts. He has also noticed that some teachers are engaging students in the critique of writing more than ever before, using the common rubrics as part of the discussion.

At Ocean View Elementary School (Norfolk, Virginia), teachers use a specific writing process that builds on students' knowledge of spoken and written language to plan, compose, revise, edit, and publish (http://www2.ed.gov/programs/nclbbrs/ 2008/profiles/oceanview.pdf). In fifth grade, teachers and students use the district common writing rubric to prepare for the state's Standards of Learning writing test. This example is just another way that data analysis (accompanied by decisive teacher actions) has propelled Ocean View to the level of success that it now enjoys.

Building Leadership

At Mary Beck, Ocean View, and many other schools involved in the Data Teams process, building leadership is key. Principals, assistant principals, curriculum specialists, instructional coaches, and others in administrative or teacher-leader roles must regularly collaborate with Data Teams in order for schools to make maximum gains.

Associates from The Center consistently recommend two specific actions for building principals: (1) Review the minutes from every Data Teams meeting and

(2) meet at least once monthly with Data Teams leaders. When principals (and in some cases, other building administrators, like assistant principals or deans) commit to these two actions, Data Teams are simply more effective. *It's the monitoring that makes the difference.* Just as teachers monitor progress made toward goals for students in their classes, administrators need to monitor the progress of Data Teams.

Building administrators sometimes monitor the work of the teams more closely than just by reviewing and/or commenting on the minutes and meeting with the Data Teams leaders. If particular teams are struggling, administrators can visit those meetings in an attempt to improve the quality of the meetings or to influence the decisions that are made. The leadership skills of the administrator are very important in such a situation. Because Data Teams are teacher-driven, an administrator must walk the fine line between being inquisitive, supportive, and gently challenging and being directive.

In some buildings, additional personnel used as ad hoc Data Teams members can also make a tremendous difference. For example, at Warren Harding High School (Bridgeport, Connecticut), the literacy coach and mathematics coach attend Data Teams meetings of various subjects and offer support as teachers determine instructional strategies. Instructional coaches utilized in this fashion are instrumental in helping teachers refine their strategies, select content-area texts, and orchestrate the strategies, sometimes modeling or co-teaching.

Administrators and coaches alike must be prepared for common challenges in the early implementation stages of Data Teams. The group development stages first proposed by Tuckman (1965) have been helpful to some Data Teams leaders and administrators with whom The Center has worked. These stages are forming, storming, norming, and performing. Any group, when first formed, is polite and congenial and is generally unsure of its tasks and roles. In this stage, it is helpful for administrators to be very hands-on and directive, making sure that each team starts the work with a sense of purpose and mission, clear expectations, and a basic understanding of the five steps and different roles.

The storming stage usually comes next. The length of this period differs by team based on the personalities and perspectives of the team members. Storming involves the team trying to complete its work; therefore, confusion about what data to monitor, how to create and use assessments, and the steps of the process is common. Building administrators, coaches, and other teacher-leaders, including Data Teams leaders, may need to be more involved with and directive of some teams in this stage than with others—and should be forewarned that a very few Data Teams may remain in this stage for an entire school year.

The third stage is norming. In this stage, members of a Data Team have become accustomed to working with each other. The team completes all five steps in each meeting and enacts common instructional strategies with success. Team members have certain roles and responsibilities and are "in the groove" of doing the work. In this stage, however, individual members may become uncomfortable at some point and return to storming behavior.

The highest stage of functioning is performing. This stage is exemplified by interdependence and excellent results. Data Teams that are in the performing stage can serve as positive examples to others; skillful leaders should find ways to highlight and replicate their practices.

Joann Elder, a teacher in Elkhart Community Schools, captures the evolution of Data Teams eloquently:

> At first the Data Teams process seemed cumbersome and not connected to what we were teaching. Once we were able to understand the connection between our data and our teaching, the process took on new meaning. Now, we use the data to drive what we teach. As teachers, we don't often get to see the results of our teaching. We aren't really sure if our students learned anything. With our data, we know not only if our students learned something, we know who did and who didn't. I feel like I know the strengths and weaknesses of all of my students. I don't have to guess anymore; I know what they are (personal communication, February 2010).

Principals (like Lauren Campsen at Ocean View Elementary) who help to create and sustain a culture focused on data analysis as a necessary and ongoing part of increasing achievement experience the best results from the Data Teams model. Schools that make appreciable gains in literacy by employing a Data Teams model do so also by having high engagement from the administrators on campus.

The Ongoing Impact of Data Teams: A Vignette

In Elkhart, Indiana, Riverview Elementary School is a grades K–6 school of approximately 340 students with a free- or reduced-lunch-eligibility rate of 69 percent—up from 27 percent in 2001. Just over 50 percent of students are white, a shift from 82 percent in 2001. In addition to the half of the students who are white, Riverview currently has an enrollment of 24 percent Hispanic students, 11 percent multiracial students, and 8 percent black students. Approximately 22 percent of Riverview students are ELLs. The teaching staff is fairly stable with an average teacher age of forty-five. The school had an overall passing rate of 66 percent on the ISTEP (state test) in 2009, up from 62 percent the previous year, and is working hard in the current year to improve even more. The work of the Data Teams is instrumental, and several teams have experienced dramatic results.

The kindergarten team at Riverview has realized some very important successes as their students learn basic literacy skills. In the spring of 2009, the team assessed students on whether or not they could correctly sequence events in a story that had been read orally. Initially, 45 percent of students could meet the standard. On the post-assessment of this same skill, 82 percent of students were proficient. This team continues to work together effectively and to help their kindergarten students reach significant milestones in early literacy.

Across town, the first-grade team at Bristol Elementary School is closely monitoring student writing as part of its Data Teams work. Recently the team found that students were improving in some areas represented on the rubric but were also continuing to show misunderstanding of (or weakness in) a few key writing skills. How did these team members respond? They revised the existing rubric to make a more succinct, student-friendly, focused rubric with the following required for proficiency in a written piece:

- A clear main idea

- Four or more details supporting the main idea

- A beginning, middle, and end

- Four or more sentences, all with capital letters for the first words and end marks at the end

- Correct spelling of sight words

Team members then planned to go back to a set of papers that they had just collected from students, apply the new streamlined criteria, confer with students, and apply instructional strategies specifically to areas in which students showed the greatest need.

Data Teams at work—at Riverview, and at Bristol, and at numerous other campuses all over the United States and abroad—are doing thousands of students a great service when they advance the literacy of those students.

References

Adelman, C. 2004. *Principal Indicators of Student Academic Histories in Postsecondary Education, 1972–2000.* Washington, D.C.: U.S. Department of Education.

Ainsworth, L. 2003. *Power Standards: Identifying the Standards That Matter the Most.* Englewood, CO: Lead + Learn Press.

Allington, R.L., and P.M. Cunningham. 2010. *Classrooms That Work: They Can All Read and Write,* fifth edition. Upper Saddle River, NJ: Allyn and Bacon.

Bardo, D. February 2010. Personal communication (electronic mail message).

Biancarosa, G., and C. Snow. 2004. *Reading Next: A Vision for Action and Research in Middle and High School Literacy.* Washington, D.C.: Alliance for Excellent Education. Available at http://www.all4ed.org/publications/ReadingNext/ReadingNext.pdf.

Blue Ribbon Schools Program: 2008 School Profile, Ocean View Elementary School. Available at http://www2.ed.gov/programs/nclbbrs/2008/profiles/oceanview.pdf.

Bouchard, B. February 2010. Personal communication (electronic mail message).

Elder, J. February 2010. Personal communication (electronic mail message).

Elkhart Community Schools. 2009. *Writing Handbook.* Available at http://elkhart.k12.in.us/3_staff/curric/development/Writing%20Handbook.pdf.

Graham, S., and D. Perin. 2007. "A Meta-Analysis of Writing Instruction for Adolescent Students." *Journal of Educational Psychology*, vol. 99, pp. 445–476.

Haycock, K. 2010. "Achievement in America: A Quick Look at What the Numbers Tell Us." Presentation at the Aspen Institute in Wye, Maryland. Available at http://www.edtrust.org/print/1412.

Hill, J. August. 2009. "One Year's Results, Five Years of Work. Elkhart Community Schools." Elkhart, IN.

———. February 2010. Personal communication (electronic mail message).

Jackson, D. March 2008. Personal communication (electronic mail message).

Leadership and Learning Center. 2009. White Paper Series: Bristol Public Schools, Bristol, Connecticut. Available at http://www.leadandlearn.com/files/file/white-paper/Bristol-White-Paper.pdf.

———. 2010. "Virginia School Drives Up Achievement." Available at http://leadandlearn.com/edgov-article.

Lonigan, C.J., and T.N.D. Shanahan. n.d. *Executive Summary: Developing Early Literacy; Report of the National Early Literacy Panel.* Jessup, MD: National Institute for Literacy. Available at http://www.nifl.gov/publications/pdf/NELPSummary.pdf.

National Center for Education Statistics. 2007. *Literacy Behind Bars: Results from the 2003 National Assessment of Adult Literacy Prison Survey.* Available at http://nces.ed.gov/pubs2007/2007473_1.pdf.

National Institute for Literacy. 2001. *Fast Facts on Literacy.* Quoted in the Humboldt Literacy Project. Available at http://www.eurekawebs.com/humlit/fast_facts.htm.

No Child Left Behind (NCLB) School Report: 2007–2008 School Year. Bristol School District. Available at http://www.csde.state.ct.us/public/cedar/nclb/dist_school_nclb_results/2007-08/01_99/17_bristol_district.pdf.

Ocean View Elementary School. 2008. Available at http://www2.ed.gov/programs/nclbbrs/2008/profiles/oceanview.pdf.

Patriot High School. 2009. "School Accountability Report Card." Available at http://www.jusd.k12.ca.us/cnt/docs/Phs0708.pdf.

Reeves, D.B. 2010. "21st Century Skills Reconsidered—Technology as Master or Tool?" Presentation, Marco Island, FL. Available at http://www.leadandlearn.com/doug-presentations-1/.

Schmoker, M. 2006. *Results Now: How We Can Achieve Unprecedented Improvements in Teaching and Learning.* Alexandria, VA: ASCD.

———. 2009. The Opportunity: From Brutal Facts to the Best Schools We've Ever Had. Presentation, UASCD Conference, Provo, UT. Available at http://www.slideshare.net/justinreeve/the-opportunityfrom-brutal-facts-to-the-best-schools-weve-ever-had.

Tuckman, B.W. 1965. "Development Sequence in Small Groups." *Psychological Bulletin,* no. 63, pp. 384–399.

White, S. 2007. "Research from the Field: Data Teams." Unpublished report shared at retreat sponsored by The Leadership and Learning Center.

Instruction and the
Real Value of Data Teams

A PRACTICAL LENS

> "...what teachers do
>
> matters."
>
> HATTIE, 2009*

Dr. Michael White tells a wonderful story of the transformation of a teacher through the Data Teams process. As he says, teachers feel empowered in the Data Teams process as they are collaboratively making instructional decisions and plans to meet the needs of their learners. Teams use an explicit process that allows teachers to focus on learning, and also to focus on teaching.

Collaborative dialogue allows teachers to go "beyond the numbers" and dig into the root causes of student learning. Dr. White describes a process that a Data Team used in order to better meet the needs of the learners in their classrooms. **How does your team currently collaborate? How could you incorporate Dr. White's best practices and recommendations to further accelerate the teaching and learning of your team?**

*Hattie, J. 2009. *Visible Learning: A Synthesis of Over 800 Meta-Analyses Relating to Achievement.* New York, NY: Routledge, p. 23.

CHAPTER 3

Instruction and the Real Value of Data Teams

MICHAEL WHITE, Ph.D.

We need to embrace a way of doing business that combines pragmatism, idealism, and the bottom line— student achievement.

I am not telling you anything you don't know when I say that too many students are taught by middling teachers in middling or worse schools. The only question is: How long can we get away with running schools this way? We may be about to find out! After years of dancing around the issue, politicians, parents, and pundits are tired of waiting for us to catch up. No longer content to play "don't ask, don't tell," they want to know which teachers produce the best and worst students.

"Adequate yearly progress," "peer review," "value added," and "corrective actions" are terms, or threats, that did not exist a few years ago, but today they influence our day-to-day work. More changes seem likely. And chances are the next set of changes will be bolder and probably make No Child Left Behind seem comparatively mild.

Don't want to be nagged? Don't want to change? Sorry, but this can no longer be about what we want. It's about what we need to do to achieve the best results possible for the children entrusted to us each year. We need to embrace a way of doing business that combines pragmatism, idealism, and the bottom line— student achievement.

We need to change because the world has changed. The recent past has shown us that a good education beats a big house or big portfolio every time. And unless we get more students through high school and through college or vocational programs, no bank bailout, stimulus package, or cash-for-clunkers program will be enough to regain our prosperity. And if the day when a high school education would serve a graduate for a lifetime is gone, then the margin of error for teachers in this new economy is also gone. Knowledge— the stuff jobs are made of, no matter the economy— is a person's most valuable asset. And that makes teachers more important than ever. Extraordinary teachers could be the most potent antipoverty program in the country.

Those who want to keep their jobs and also be good at them—and hopefully that would include all of us—must admit how important we are. Let's also admit that extraordinary teaching is not an easy or individual accomplishment: It is the result of common sense, common instruction, common assessment, and, most importantly, collaboration. Boatloads of schools have proven that extraordinary teaching occurs when teachers team up to improve student learning beyond what any individual teacher could achieve alone (Darling–Hammond, 2010; Reeves, 2004; Schmoker, 2006).

Real collaboration, not the coffee klatch and doughnut kind, can be scary! However, we shouldn't get too nervous—collaboration is less about attaining perfection and more about being a better teacher today than we were yesterday, about acknowledging imperfection and looking for competency and complementaries among our colleagues. Regardless of its name—Data Team, child-study group, or Professional Learning Community—collaboration allows us to magnify our strengths and work with other teachers who provide different but equally important strengths. You may be a ninja at number sense but not an expert on geometry. But the teacher across the hall cannot wait to share her engaging activity for scalene and isosceles triangles. While no single person will possess every dimension of an extraordinary teacher, the team is more likely to have all of those qualities. And when we come together and talk about teaching, we discover that we have the capacity right now to raise student achievement and that improvement is something we can generate, rather than sitting around waiting for it to be Power-Pointed out to us by so-called experts.

What makes Data Teams so powerful? All of the following: the collecting and charting of data, the setting of goals, the analysis of student strengths and weaknesses, and the refinement of instruction and intervention. But the big story boiling beneath the charting, the assessments, and the instruction might be the changes that take place within individual teachers. They begin to expect more from themselves, their peers, and their students. Small wins and shared successes take the place of the notion that some children and some teachers are destined to fail. Data Teams are not only powerful, they are empowering.

Let's take a look at the impact of a Data Team on an individual.

Beginning at the Beginning: Opening Day

As we join our fourth-grade teacher, Ken Tankerous, he is walking into the high school auditorium where this year's opening day celebration is being held.

> **Ken:** If I sit in the back, I can get to the car and back to the building quickly. Twenty years, and it's always the same thing: our superintendent telling us how our kids did on the state test and prodding everyone to do better. How about telling us how? Does he think I've been saving a better lesson plan until he caught me?
>
> I have more students than I've ever had before. They have lots of labels, too. It's like alphabet soup with all those IEPs and IATs. Often, it's all just an excuse for not doing the work as far as I'm concerned. I already know what my data will show—kids don't care and neither do their parents. And the parents who *are* involved spend all of their time making excuses for their kids, asking me to bend the rules, and complaining about my inflexibility.
>
> My lessons have always worked just fine for the kids who want to learn and do the work. It's not my fault the others aren't motivated. I'm an educator, not an edutainer. I get paid to teach. I have the textbook that the board of education adopted, and that's what I'm going to teach.

First Data Teams Meeting Ever

• Analyze state test data and determine priority standards and skills.

> **Ken:** Well, this is embarrassing. My students scored low on reading comprehension again this year, but the two other fourth-grade classes did better. Maybe that literacy intervention program that Ira and Kay used really works. They were really excited about the results they were seeing by midterm last year. I should have jumped on board then. Maybe during these meetings I can learn exactly what they were doing.
>
> The good news is, last year's group of students did really well on most of the content of the state tests. Bad news: We missed a lot of points

on the extended-response questions. Measurement was an area of weakness in mathematics. This was true across the district, so I'm sure that those are two of the areas we will focus on as a team.

We all agreed to spend an extra week on measurement, and we've planned for more opportunities for students to write responses to questions and score them themselves with rubrics.

Kay and I had low scores in geometry, too. Kay actually admitted that she didn't really have time to get through the book last year and just skimmed the geometry section. Then I confessed that geometry has never been my strong suit. Ira showed us a lesson he does with the game Battleship. Heck, I can use his game boards and do that lesson, too. He's also going to share all of his geometry class notes with us.

Meeting Two: Determining When to Teach

• Develop a calendar for the priority standards and skills.
• Create or select pre-assessments.

> **Ken:** At first I wasn't sure if I could be locked into teaching stuff at the same time Kay and Ira are teaching it. Why do we need a calendar when we all have the same textbook? Basically, I already have my year planned out. If we teach the book, we're bound to hit most of the standards.
>
> Ira and Kay think that our meetings will probably be better if we're teaching the same thing at about the same time. Kay will have the hardest time staying with the calendar. Last year I think she spent two weeks making papier-maché pumpkins for Halloween. That's probably why she never gets to geometry!
>
> Pre-assessments—I never heard of anything so stupid! Testing students before we teach them the lesson is a waste of time. Of course they aren't going to get the questions right. I'm not going to waste any of my quarterly test questions for this. Kay thinks that we can use the district's quarterly assessments as our pre-assessments, too. At least that will save us from having to write new questions.

Ira believes that using a pre- and post-assessment model will allow us to show how effective our Data Teams are becoming. I wonder if Ira thinks that will get us a raise.

Meeting Three: Determining How to Teach

- Analyze pre-assessment results.
- Develop a lesson.

Ken: What the "h," "e," "double hockey sticks" is going on? The pre-assessment was an easy fraction question:

> Heidi and James each have a bottle of juice that is the same size. Heidi drank 1/4 of her juice. James drank 1/3 of his juice. Who drank more juice? Use pictures, words, or numbers to show how you know.

Loads of kids answered like this:

Heidi drank more because 4 is bigger than 3

These kids don't know the difference between fractions and whole numbers! I would never have thought to start my lesson here, but starting anywhere else would mean that these kids would be lost.

Kay has a good idea for our lesson. She wants to introduce the lesson by incorporating our students' misconceptions about fractions and whole numbers. She also thinks we should read *Gator Pie* by Louise Matthews to the class. The book is about two alligators finding a pie in the swamp. They decide to divide it and are pleased to see how much they will each receive. But a bigger alligator comes out of the swamp and demands pie, so they have to cut it into thirds. The story progresses with more alligators coming out of the swamp and demanding part of the pie. It's a silly story, but my kids will love it. A few years ago I read to my students all the time. I need to start doing that again.

I volunteered to take the lowest students from all three classes and do a pre-activity if Ira helps me develop it. Truth is, I'm starting to think that Ira is an OK guy, and Kay is fun once you get past that denim vest with the apple patches all over it.

Our lesson looks pretty solid. We will start by asking students to demonstrate and predict in their math journals using the following prompts.

> Draw a diagram to show how you would divide a pie for two people, three people, four people, and eight people. Predict what will happen to the pieces of pie if you were to continue to divide it among more people. What happened to the pieces of pie as you divided the pie into more and more pieces? What happened to the denominator of the fraction as you divided the pie into more pieces?

Meeting Four: After Instruction

• Review post-assessment data.

• Determine interventions for students who did not meet goal.

> **Ken:** My class did pretty well. On the pre-assessment, I had 68 percent of my students failing, but on the post-test, only 8 percent failed. My class improved the most!

> Now we're going to plan what to do with the kids who are still struggling. I was surprised to see how many interventions Kay and Ira actually have in place. Ira uses a box of math activities for struggling kids, and Kay uses a parent volunteer to reteach skills. Parents love Kay. Kay also has intervention scripts written out so that her volunteers can deliver the intervention effectively. I didn't mention that my usual intervention was a call to the psychologist to see about getting a kid tested.

At this point it might be tempting to categorize our colleagues as Kens, Iras, or Kays, but we won't. Teachers are much more complicated than the short caricatures created here. The truth is, if we look closely, we would see a bit of Ken, Kay, and Ira in all of us. The important thing is to see how Data Teams allow individual teachers to learn and grow. And isn't that what schools are—places for students and teachers to learn and grow?

The idea of teachers like Ken, Kay, and Ira helping each other is so obviously sensible that it never goes away, but it is so very threatening to the status quo that it's never implemented deeply, broadly, and consistently over time. We value teaching our students to work together and to learn from one another, but we don't model this behavior for them. We sing the praises of two heads being better than one, while we ignore the expertise of our colleagues across the hall.

We expect to hone our skills while incarcerated in a cafeteria for eight hours of mandatory , districtwide professional development. After these events, it is the norm for each of us to trudge back to our rooms to work in isolation like independent contractors, sharing only the refrigerator and the parking lot. Each classroom is its own "microcosm."

Collaboration takes work and intentionality. It's unrealistic to think that you can flip your school to this type of behavior overnight. Knowing what to do next is always harder than knowing what to do. Here are a few next steps that will encourage active collaboration:

- Approach teachers whose skills you respect, and ask them to observe your teaching and offer some suggestions on your methods. This takes courage!

- Ask to sit in on the class of a teacher you respect. Say something as simple as, "I always hear students leaving your class still discussing what you taught. I'd love to see how you get that level of engagement. Do you mind if I sit in on one of your classes to observe?" Or, "I noticed that your students mastered this week's indicator. What are you doing?"

- Ask colleagues about conferences or workshops that they've attended. Mention an article you've read that they may find interesting. Share a brochure on a workshop in another teacher's area of expertise.

- Don't think that because you are the "rookie" you have nothing to contribute. The flow of information doesn't always go from experienced teacher to new teacher. Just as you value the child in your class who asks pertinent questions, your questions are essential to your growth and to that of your colleagues. Your questions encourage more experienced teachers to consider practices and the basis for them. You are also likely to hold the most current knowledge of cutting-edge educational research that can and should be discussed as well as well-developed information-gathering skills.

- And if you and your colleagues are initially reluctant to talk about student achievement, common assessments, and lessons, you may find it safer to discuss and collaborate on student behavioral issues like reducing the number of office referrals or the number of bus incidents. So start there!

Once you have started or revived a Data Team in your school, remember—

simple plans work best. Here is a modest suggestion for activities in which your Data Teams could engage:

- Develop common understandings of the standards and your state tests.
- Analyze student data on the state test or quarterly tests.
- Select exemplars to share.
- Identify lessons for remediation or enrichment.
- Develop common assessments in order to plan and evaluate instruction.
- Collaboratively score student work.
- Identify lessons and materials for remediation or enrichment.

Conclusion

When historians get around to listing the most astonishing discoveries about student achievement, there are two findings that won't make their list:

1. An effective teacher has more impact on student achievement than all other factors combined (White, et al., 2009).

2. When teachers get together to talk in concrete, precise language about instruction and student work, their teaching dramatically improves and student achievement rises (Schmoker, 2006).

Sadly, what might make our historians' list of astonishing discoveries is that we knew it was all about teaching and collaboration, yet we rarely collaborated in our schools. And while we frequently challenged the status quo, we never pushed long enough or hard enough to change it.

References

Darling–Hammond, L. 2010. *The Flat World of Education: How America's Commitment to Equity Will Determine Our Future.* New York: Teachers College Press.

Matthews, L. 1995. *Gator Pie.* Boston, MA: Sundance Publishing.

Reeves, D.B. 2004. *Accountability in Action: A Blueprint for Learning Organizations,* second edition. Sample chapters are available for free at the Web site: www.MakingStandardsWork.com.

Schmoker, M. 2006. *Results Now: How We Can Achieve Unprecedented Improvements in Teaching and Learning.* Alexandria, VA: ASCD.

White, M., et al. 2009. *Extraordinary Teachers: Teaching for Success.* Englewood, CO: Lead + Learn Press.

SECTION 2

Data Teams
for
All Learners

Response to Intervention Joins Data Teams

A PRACTICAL LENS

"...RTI has the potential to help transform schools if the educators within them embrace the big ideas of a professional learning community: a commitment to high levels of learning for all students, a commitment to a collaborative culture, and a commitment to using results to foster continuous improvement."

DUFOUR, DUFOUR, EAKER, KARHANEK, 2010*

Dr. Linda Gregg clearly describes the relationship of Response to Intervention (RTI) and the Data Teams process. Through "Melissa's Story," Dr. Gregg illustrates how teachers collaboratively used interdependent processes (RTI and Data Teams) to close the gaps and accelerate student learning.

Schools have systematic processes in place to provide interventions for students. Dr. Gregg shows us how structured collaboration increases the impact of the intervention process. **What does your current intervention process look like? How can schools use RTI and Data Teams as interdependent processes, rather than as independent initiatives?**

*DuFour, R., R. DuFour, R. Eaker, and G. Karhanek. 2010. *Raising the Bar and Closing the Gap: Whatever It Takes.* Bloomington, IN: Solution Tree, pp. 20–21.

CHAPTER 4

Response to Intervention Joins Data Teams

LINDA GREGG, Ed.D.

Using Response to Intervention as early as possible will help school districts to avoid the massive gaps that can appear when students are left to "fall between the cracks."

Introduction

Response to Intervention (RTI) is a dynamic complement to the Data Teams process. In this chapter, you will learn about the relationship between Data Teams and RTI. You will have an opportunity to see an example of the Data Teams process in relation to RTI by reading a short student profile that depicts a fifth-grade student. You will follow a problem-solving process for the Data Team and learn how appropriate interventions are selected. In addition, you will see how to monitor the student's progress with regard to intervention.

Background

In 2004, as a result of the reauthorization of the Individuals with Disabilities Education Improvement Act (IDEIA), the federal government provided an opportunity for school districts across the country to make a determination of students with Specific Learning Disabilities (SLDs) based on a discrepancy model and/or the students' response to scientifically research-based instruction from highly qualified teachers.

According to IDEIA (614, b, 6, A, B 2):

(A) When determining whether a child has a Specific Learning Disability as defined in section 602, a Local Education Agency

(LEA) shall not be required to take into consideration whether a child has a severe discrepancy between achievement and intellectual ability in oral expression, listening comprehension, written expression, basic reading skill, reading comprehension, mathematical calculation, or mathematical reasoning. (B) Additionally, in determining whether a child has a Specific Learning Disability, a local educational agency [LEA, or school district] may use a process that determines whether the child responds to scientific, research-based interventions as a part of the evaluation procedures.

The key components of RTI suggested by the federal government include but are not limited to:

- Universal screening of academics and behavior
- High-quality, research-based classroom instruction
- Implementation of appropriate research-based interventions
- Student assessment with a classroom focus
- Continuous progress monitoring during interventions
- Teaching behavior–fidelity measures

Response to Intervention Defined

RTI is a framework that guides instruction for *all* students. There are multiple definitions of RTI, including, but not limited to, the following:

Response to Intervention is the practice of providing high-quality instruction and interventions matched to student need, monitoring progress frequently to make decisions about changes in instruction or goals, and applying student response data to important educational decisions. RTI should be applied to decisions in general education, remedial education, and special education. The goal is to create a well-integrated system of instruction and intervention guided by data on student outcome (National Association of State Directors of Special Education [NASDSE], 2008).

The primary paradigm shift seen in RTI is to consider the achievement of *all* students, not just the struggling learner. The government suggests early intervention as a critical component of RTI. School districts have introduced RTI in a variety of ways. In some cases, the introduction has included pre-kindergarten through grade 2 students only, and in other cases, kindergarten through grade 6 only. Currently, numerous middle schools and high schools are also using RTI, thus broadening the use of early intervention from kindergarten to twelfth grade as originally intended. A major benefit to early intervention is to avoid the massive gaps that appear when students fall between the cracks. Early intervention can help the teacher take steps to provide both academic and behavioral intervention strategies immediately. RTI also actively involves parents and the community.

Multi-Tiered Intervention

School districts across the country use different terminology to describe a tiered process of RTI. For purposes of this chapter, the following terms will be used for the RTI tiers of intervention: Tier 1 (universal) interventions are provided to all students in the classroom. They should be high quality, research-based strategies. Tier 2 (targeted) interventions are implemented when student assessment indicates

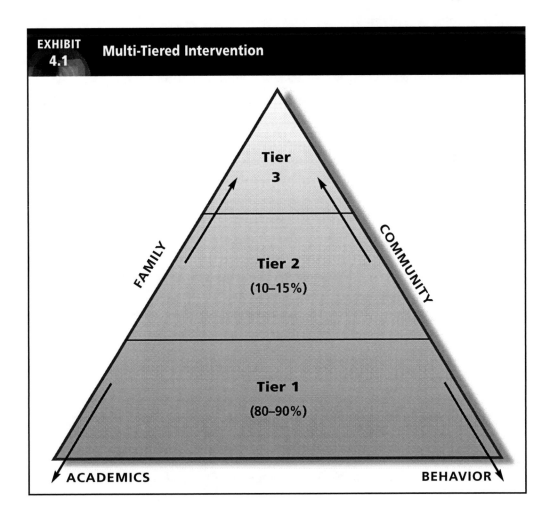

EXHIBIT 4.1 **Multi-Tiered Intervention**

Tier 3

Tier 2 (10–15%)

Tier 1 (80–90%)

FAMILY

COMMUNITY

ACADEMICS

BEHAVIOR

that a student is not responding from Tier 1 instruction and not making adequate gains from universal instruction alone. Tier 3 (intensive) interventions are provided by highly structured, intentional, systematic, and explicit instruction in an area of assessed need. Typically, the duration and intensity of the intervention are increased to meet the needs of the student and to accelerate student response.

Three tiers of intervention are represented in an inverted triangle or may be described as a pyramid similar to the one shown in Exhibit 4.1. Response to Intervention addresses the academic and behavioral issues for individual and groups of students. RTI involves all children, kindergarten through grade 12, in general education, special education, gifted and talented, and English language learners (ELL) programs. The key is to make sure that students have an opportunity to succeed to the best of their ability.

The three tiers in Exhibit 4.1 represent the percentage of students typically seen in each tier. At the beginning of the school year, when the first universal screening is administered (prior to instruction), the percentages in the pyramid may appear top heavy, with a much higher number of students needing targeted and intensive interventions. Districts beginning the RTI process should consider the importance of a strong Tier 1 program of high-quality, research-based instruction and differentiation to meet the needs of all students. Students who do not respond as expected to Tier 1 intervention strategies may require targeted interventions at Tier 2, and students who do not respond as expected in Tier 2 may require intensive interventions at Tier 3. The Data Teams problem-solving process for RTI can help the team address small-group and individual student needs.

Student Profile

Melissa is a fifth-grade student identified by the Data Team as a student requiring Tier 2 intervention strategies. In this section, you will have the opportunity to experience the conversations held with Melissa's classroom teacher, mother, and the members of the Data Team.

Melissa, Grade 5

Melissa is an enthusiastic student. She loves school and has near-perfect attendance. Her favorite subjects are art, music, mathematics, and science. She receives high scores in each of these subjects. Her parents are very proud of her. During a recent parent–teacher conference, Melissa's mother, Mrs. Peterson, indicated that she and her husband are becoming increasingly concerned regarding Melissa's language arts and social studies classes. Ms. Griego, Melissa's fifth-grade teacher, stated that indeed she has noticed that Melissa's scores are consistently below proficiency in these two subjects. Mrs. Peterson was aware of this and is becoming increasingly concerned that the gap continues to grow, causing a serious decline in the grades in Melissa's content classes. Melissa uses context clues and takes advantage of visuals and hand-on activities to perform well in her science class.

Ms. Griego was not acutely aware that Melissa's scores had declined so sharply. Melissa is a delightful student. She is cooperative and works hard in all of her classes. Ms. Griego told Melissa's mother that she would address the issue immediately. A grade-level Data Team meeting was already scheduled in two days, and Ms. Griego promised to analyze Melissa's scores and seek suggestions for intervention

---

EXHIBIT 4.2 **Sample Results of the Reading Assessment**

Teacher: Ms. Griego

School: Eagle Elementary School

Grade: Fifth

Date of Assessment: October 28

Assessment: Curriculum-Based Measurement (CBM) Language Arts: Reading Comprehension

Proficient: 4.8–5.0+
Close to Proficient: 4.0–4.7
Significantly Below Proficient: 3.9 and below

Students:

Melissa	4.0	4.5
DeWayne	4.8	3.3
Marina	4.7	2.9
Katrina	4.9	2.6
Carmine	5.3	7.5
Jesus	3.0	3.5
Keisha	4.8	5.0
Jared	4.5	2.3
Blake	5.0	4.2
Miguel	3.8	2.0
Faye	5.5	4.0

strategies from her colleagues. Mrs. Peterson was very happy to hear the plan and said that she would help Ms. Griego and Melissa as much as possible.

On Wednesday afternoon at 3:10, the fifth-grade Data Team members met. There were four teachers on the fifth-grade team. The team leader, Ms. North, called the meeting on time and asked if the timekeeper, Mr. Sange, could keep them on a schedule for forty-five minutes. He agreed and also began taking notes as formal documentation of the meeting. Ms. Anderson, another fifth-grade teacher, discussed the results of the latest common formative assessment (CFA) in reading. The scores for Melissa's classes may be seen in Exhibit4. 2.

Although the scores in Exhibit 4.2 represent Ms. Griego's classroom, the scores for all four teachers were discussed during the Data Team meeting. The teachers had provided a reading comprehension test from their fifth-grade curriculum to students as a pre-assessment. The fifth-grade team noticed that many of the students were having difficulty with content-specific vocabulary on the fifth-grade level.

The fifth-grade team members were relatively new to the Data Teams problem-solving process. They had begun in September with a meeting to discuss norms and to assign roles. The team firmly believed that the use of the Data Teams process could help them focus on the needs of individual students and of small groups of students and provide appropriate research-based instructional strategies for all students. The team members also noticed that there were at least two to three students in each of their classes who scored close to proficient on the pre-assessment. The team discussed the need to continue to differentiate and provide high-quality, research-based instruction for students who scored in the proficient range. The fifth-grade team also pointed out the need to provide intensive intervention strategies for the students who scored significantly below proficiency in the comprehension assessment. For purposes of this example of Tier 2, the team will continue to discuss Melissa and students who scored close to proficient, thus requiring targeted intervention.

Ms. Griego briefly shared what she had discussed with Melissa's mother, Mrs. Peterson, during the parent–teacher conference. Mr. Sange, another fifth-grade teacher, mentioned a similar conversation with two of his parents. The team members looked at several items on their state standards and state-mandated tests and recognized that vocabulary across the curriculum for fifth-graders was weighted very high on the state-mandated assessments. Ms. Jones, the literacy coach (who regularly joins Data Teams meetings at two assigned schools on a bi-monthly basis), told the team that it is not uncommon for students to miss several items on the test due to a misunderstanding of the vocabulary.

Ms. Griego, asked Ms. Jones for more clarification of this issue. Some of the examples provided by Ms. Jones for mathematics included a difference in expression; e.g., times tables versus multiplication or take-away versus subtraction, and knowledge of terms of operation, such as dividend, quotient, divisor, and difference. She also indicated that students were struggling with directions and expectations. In social studies, terms of geography taught in class did not match terms used in wider contexts.

The instructional coach said that it is very difficult to see students miss a question merely because a different, unfamiliar term was used. According to Ms. Jones, teachers at all grade levels frequently lament that they know they have taught the concept or content and are horrified to see that students missed these questions on the state- or district-mandated assessments. They were convinced that the students knew the information, but application and generalization of the information was not firm. The students even scored well on the formative classroom assessments. Students recognized the vocabulary in a sentence or in the context of a

EXHIBIT 4.3	Problem-Solving Analysis

Data Analysis

Problem Statement: Four of fifteen students in the fifth-grade class scored below proficiency in core content-specific vocabulary.

Strengths: Cooperative, good attendance, willing to learn new things. Strong skills in other academic areas.	**Inferences:** Positive work habits. Limited background knowledge of abstract vocabulary words. Difficulty generalizing words in a variety of settings.
Challenges: Gaps in background knowledge. Low comprehension of abstract vocabulary terms.	**Inferences:** Students appear to be visual learners. Abstract concepts have not been identified.
Tier Level: 2	**Rationale:** At Tier 1, several intervention strategies were used for differentiation, including but not limited to graphic organizers, pre-teaching vocabulary, computer practice, specific vocabulary homework, and study buddies, but these strategies were unsuccessful. Students did not meet expectations with Tier 1 interventions.

story. All of the teachers indicated that they have a common vocabulary list and use standard language when teaching, but some students are still unable to apply the new words in multiple ways.

The Data Team members realized that collecting and charting the pre-assessment scores (Step 1) was helpful. However, in order to determine which intervention strategies they should use to assist the students with their vocabulary skills, they needed to professionally analyze the data (Step 2) to determine the root cause of the students' performance. Exhibit 4.3 is a synopsis of their analysis of Melissa and other students in Ms. Griego's class. It is possible to analyze individual students and targeted groups of students during this process. (A template for problem-solving analysis [Exhibit 4.7] is provided in the Additional Resources section at the end of this chapter.)

After reviewing and analyzing the comprehension scores and discussing the strengths and challenges and making several inferences based on the data, the team decided that one root cause of the problem was comprehension of abstract vocabulary. The fifth-grade team wrote a goal (Step 3) for the students, whom they felt, based on the data, were very close to proficiency but needed targeted intervention to help them. This goal is shown in Exhibit 4.4.

EXHIBIT 4.4   SMART Goal

Eighty-five percent of the fifth-grade students scoring below proficiency will achieve a score of proficient or higher within the next two weeks for content-specific vocabulary.

The criteria used to write the goal are the same as described elsewhere in this book for the Data Teams process. The goal should be specific, measurable, achievable, relevant, and timely. During this step the team should work together to determine the root cause through a careful analysis of all available data.

The building administrator, Ms. Sugarman, entered the team meeting about fifteen minutes into the forty-five-minute session to observe the process and to monitor the recommendations for interventions that she would be observing in classrooms throughout the coming two weeks. Ms. Sugarman raised a very important question to the Data Team regarding Response to Intervention. She wanted to know if the team had placed Melissa and the other students in the Tier 2 level immediately based on the results of one pre-assessment. The team leader, Ms. North, explained that the students had been given multiple assessments with at least three data points and that the team-had made a trend-line analysis before moving their students to Tier 2 or Tier 3.

The team members explained to Ms. North that they give the students common formative assessments (pre and post) to determine the students' content knowledge and skills. They analyze the results of the pre-assessment and make sure that the selected instructional strategies are scientifically research based and are designed to match individual student needs before they move students to another tier level. Additionally, the team matches the prioritized standards and pacing guide to make sure that they are focused on the areas that hold the most weight for the next unit of instruction, grade level, and mandated assessments, and that they provide enduring knowledge and skill for the student. During Step 4 of the Data Teams process, the team shared several interventions that they routinely used with students at the Tier 1 level. They were happy that the majority of the students were proficient with the existing high-quality, research-based strategies. The data team decided to continue the differentiation strategies for the majority of the students. Some of those strategies may be seen in Exhibit 4.5 (page 69).

Now the team needed to discuss the other students who were not responding as expected to the Tier 1 instructional strategies. The following is a list of sample interventions that the team considered after analyzing the root cause for Melissa and a few of her classmates:

- Continue pre-teaching vocabulary (front load) prior to the group lesson.

- Create nonlinguistic representations of abstract words (student generated).

- Use a curriculum-based vocabulary computer program (focus on abstract, content-specific words) for twenty minutes, three times a day.

- Have the students attend a session with the Corps of Retired Teachers two times each week for fifteen to twenty minutes to increase their ability to comprehend the relationship between concrete words and abstract words in the content.

- Conduct a "second dose" of vocabulary (direct instruction) in a fifteen-to-twenty-minute session daily, with three to five students during a language arts station rotation with the general education teacher.

The literacy coach, Ms. Jones, felt that this list would be a good starting point but reminded the teachers that they should select only one or two of the interventions that would match the analysis. Melissa's teacher, Ms. Griego, remembered from the RTI training workshop that she had attended during the summer that the speaker stressed the importance of not supplanting direct instruction. All of the students in Ms. Griego's classes would therefore receive the core, direct instruction first (accompanied by the differentiation strategies and high-quality instruction), and then the targeted students (such as Melissa) would be given additional or supplemental instruction. Mr. Sange added that the speaker at his training session specifically had said to supplement at the Tier 2 and 3 intervention levels but not to supplant the core instruction. He also mentioned that Tier 2 can be conducted by the general-education teacher in class. This information had made a big impact on his current classroom practices. He said that, prior to attending the workshop, he would allow students to be pulled out at numerous times throughout his direct instruction of core content for assistance by tutors, therapists, and a variety of interventionists. During the direct instruction, students missed the information and would return to class, lost or confused. Students reported frustration with being pulled from class. Mr. Sange indicated that he encourages push-in supplemental assistance and often will provide the Tier 2 intervention himself during class.

Ms. Sugarman, the principal of the school, asked Mr. Sange to describe how he was able to find time to assist the students requiring Tier 2 intervention during class without the help of another adult. He shared his strategy of working with targeted students as needed during student practice, station teaching, or alternative (flex) instruction time. Also, if additional personnel or volunteers were available, supplemental instruction could take place as a brief push-in/pull-out. (Note: Transition time must be considered carefully so that instructional minutes are not lost during transitions to the activity or to a new location.) Interventionists may include but are not limited to literacy, math, or instructional coaches, a Title 1 teacher, an ELL teacher, a special-education teacher, a retired teacher, a social worker, and speech and language pathologists. Basically, it can be described as "all hands on deck." Community members may assist with guided and independent practice as well. This may include, for example, local university volunteers, approved organizations, and paraprofessionals.

Principal Sugarman said that the fifth-grade Data Team could also consult with the district's new after-school program coordinator regarding services for Melissa and a few of her other classmates. Ms. Griego told the team that Melissa's family is currently going through financial difficulties. Both parents are working, and her mother has taken on an extra job from 4:00 p.m. to midnight. Both parents feel that they can provide only limited support at home, but their daughter's education is very important to them. They promised to help in any way possible to support the school's effort to help Melissa. Melissa's parents did indicate that they could

EXHIBIT 4.5	Sample Intervention Strategies	

Sample Tier(s):	Intervention Strategies:	May Be Conducted By:
Tiers 1, 2, 3	Pre-write vocabulary on the whiteboard.	General- or special-education teacher, support staff
Tiers 1, 2, 3	Use the key words throughout the week. Have the students use the words as well in a synonym web.	General- or special-education teacher, support staff
Tiers 1, 2, 3	Create a vocabulary thesaurus.	General-education teacher, tutor, peer buddy
Tiers 1, 2, 3	Create nonlinguistic representations of abstract words.	Tutor, peer, literacy coach, support staff, tutorial
Tiers 2, 3	Use curriculum-based vocabulary on the computer three times a week for twenty minutes each time.	Computer program
Tiers 2, 3	Connect concrete to abstract words with Corps of Retired Teachers, fifteen to twenty minutes each time, two times a week.	Corps of Retired Teachers, support staff, direct instruction, tutorial

arrange to have a neighbor pick up Melissa following the after-school tutoring program three days a week from 3:15 to 5:30 p.m.

Exhibit 4.5 is a list of intervention strategies that the team members discussed during their afternoon meeting for all of the students. While their primary focus was Tier 2 during that meeting, they also listed strategies that could be used at Tiers 1 and 3. These interventions are not exclusive to a particular tier level; the decision is based on the result of the analysis of student needs.

Intervention strategies are a fluid process and may work quite well at the Tier 2 or 3 levels, but the team is cautioned not to skip the analysis (Step 2) when making the determination of which intervention to select. Ms. Sugarman reminded the

EXHIBIT
4.6
Team Meeting Notes

Student Response Team Meeting Minutes

Power Standard:

Success Criteria

Today's Date:	Date of Next Meeting:

Team Members Present:
Facilitator:
Note Taker:
Data Technician:
Timekeeper/Focus Monitor:
Active Participants:

Data Sources:

Students Below Proficient	Students Close to Proficient
Students Proficient	Students Above Proficient

SMART Goal:	Responsible for Progress Monitoring
	Targeted Scientifically Research-Based Interventions:
Percentage of ___ proficient and higher in specific standard will increase from ____ to ____ by _____ as measured by _____ given on _____.	

Evaluation of the Response to the Above Intervention

Have interventions been implemented with fidelity?
☐ Not Implemented ☐ Partially Implemented ☐ Fully Implemented

Student achievement results:

Success indicator: (evidence of actual impact on student learning):

Reasons why interventions were or were not successful:

Suggested adjustments or recommendations:

Adapted for the Data Team meeting

This fifth-grade team held its meetings on a bi-monthly basis. Ms. Griego's school decided to use the time permitted for the grade-level teams to incorporate this problem-solving process for the Data Team.

After analyzing the universal assessment results from all of the students, team members decided to focus on literacy skills during their Data Team meetings.

team members that they should consider the intervention based on the individual or on the needs of the small group and to carefully document the student's response to the intervention to determine if the student is progressing or if he or she requires additional assistance.

During the Data Team meeting, Ms. North guided the team through the steps of the team process. Mr. Sange continued to take notes of the meeting. A copy of his notes may be seen in Exhibit 4.6.

Team Meeting Steps to Problem Solve

As the Data Team members continued to develop their plans for the next two weeks of intervention for the fifth-grade students, the team leader (Ms. North) referenced a handwritten poster that was prominently displayed in the team meeting room. The items included in their poster are shown below with items specific to RTI highlighted in **bold**:

STEP 1: Conduct **universal screening** and ongoing collection of data.

- See Exhibit 4.8 (in the Additional Resources section) for a list of multiple-discipline, K–12 universal screening instruments. Exhibit 4.9 (also in the Additional Resources section) provides a template for universal assessment.

STEP 2: Analyze assessed strengths and challenges to determine the **root causes**.

- What have you observed?

- What information do the data provide?

- What are the strengths, challenges, and inferences?

- What is the root cause?

During this step of analysis, the team looked for dependent variables. When independent and dependent valuables have been identified, they will guide the team in determining which elements may be influenced or modified by intervention. The Data Team members were careful to eliminate extended discussion of items over which they had no control, such as the extent of parental participation, background knowledge, and socioeconomic status.

STEP 3: Establish SMART goals: Set, review, and revise the goals.

STEP 4: Select **scientifically research-based interventions**.

In addition to the interventions mentioned in this article, additional examples may be found in the literature listed in the references section. You may also want to access the Web sites found in Exhibit 4.8. The sites are updated frequently and provide numerous research-based interventions for team consideration.

STEP 5: **Monitor student progress during interventions.**

The Data Team members should begin to consider which method(s) they will use to monitor progress for students who are in Tier 2. This includes Melissa and two of her classmates, as well as three students in each of the other two (Mr. Sange's and Ms. North's) fifth-grade classes. The person responsible for monitoring progress should also be documented at this time.

All four teachers agreed to continue to use the Tier 1, high-quality instructional strategies and differentiation listed in Exhibit 4.5. The team also decided to begin implementation of two of the Tier 2 interventions discussed during the meeting for a period of two weeks. At the end of that time, the students would be given a post-assessment, and the results would be shared at the next Data Team meeting. The specific interventions selected will be described in the next section, "How Does It Look?" Ms. Jones, the instructional coach, indicated that she would help to monitor progress of the implementation of the strategies at least two times a week during her regular work (as literacy coach) within the fifth-grade classrooms. Ms. Jones also requested that the school administrator, Ms. Sugarman, help to monitor progress during her normal walk-throughs. She would be able to provide additional support and feedback regarding the implementation of the interventions.

How Does It Look?

The fifth-grade teachers went back to the classroom immediately and discussed their plans with the students. They wanted the students to know their scores and the plan to help them improve. They also elicited the encouragement and support of the students' parents. Mrs. Peterson, Melissa's mother, was delighted. The students were excited and also made suggestions on ways in which they could improve. One of the students for example, indicated that she felt she needed a little more time to think about the vocabulary words before being required to respond verbally or in writing. Students requiring Tier 2 interventions were told that there would be a focus on using nonlinguistic representations and working with computer-based programs three times a week during the language arts class (during independent practice time) or during the social studies class for fifteen to twenty minutes. The information on the computer would be content specific. The students in Tier 2 would study the same content as all of the other students while simultaneously developing vocabulary. Students were also given fifteen minutes during independent practice time to work with a member of the Corps of Retired Teachers the other two days a week. The students were provided with an assignment sheet that listed in the schedule the strategies that they would be using throughout the next two weeks.

How Is It Monitored?

During the regular Data Teams leadership meeting with the principal and the other grade-level Data Team members and leaders, Ms. North, the fifth-grade team leader, shared the Tier 2 intervention strategies discussed at the previous team meeting. She indicated that the classroom teachers have shared the information with the students and that they will keep a schedule and a copy of their scores. The teachers will continue to provide the Tier 1 interventions as agreed and facilitate Tier 2 for those students based on the analyzed assessment. The teachers will also ask the Corps of Retired Teachers to provide brief student progress feedback following each tutorial session. The instructional coach, Ms. Jones, will help to monitor implementation during her regular visits to the classrooms twice each week. She will look specifically for the fidelity of implementation. In the event that a teacher needs additional assistance, the coach will either demonstrate (e.g., by using nonlinguistic representations) or verbally provide coaching to help the instructor provide high-quality instruction. Additionally, the school principal, Ms. Sugarman, will help to progress monitor these specific strategies during her regular walk-throughs. The fifth-grade team leader has given a copy of the interventions that will be used and the name of the students to the principal. When Principal Sugarman visits the classrooms, she will look specifically for evidence of implementation. In the event that additional assistance is needed, the teacher will be able to consult with all of his or her colleagues during the Data Team meeting. A post-curriculum-based measurement (CBM) will be provided to the students in two weeks, and the documentation will be analyzed at the next Data Team meeting.

Summary

Response to Intervention has a direct relationship with the Data Teams process. The key differences in RTI that you may have noticed include the need for universal screening, scientifically research-based interventions, and progress monitoring. These required processes may be conducted during the regular Data Teams meeting, the Professional Learning Community (PLC) meeting, or a grade-level or department team meeting. (Note: Templates for progress monitoring reports and analysis are shown in Exhibits 4.10 and 4.11 in the section "Additional Resources" toward the end of the chapter.)

The Data Team assumes that, typically, not one individual intervention strategy will be effective for every student. The Data Team includes four stages (problem identification, problem analysis, plan implementation, and plan evaluation). It should be sensitive to individual student needs, and it depends on the fidelity of implementing interventions. Another important consideration is that the instruction should be provided by highly qualified classroom teachers. Arrangements should include parents and students as partners in the process whenever possible. Schools should follow a well-designed Response to Intervention framework and a comprehensive strategic professional development plan that includes the principles of Response to Intervention, modeling, demonstrations, collaboration, observations, coaching, and immediate feedback.

Additional Resources

EXHIBIT 4.7	Problem-Solving Analysis Form

Data Analysis

Problem statement:

Strengths:	Inferences:

Challenges:	Inferences

Tier Level:	Rationale:

Intervention:	

EXHIBIT 4.8 — Sample Universal Screening Instruments

Content	Publisher	Web Address
Early Education	Dynamic Indicators of Basic Early Literacy Skills (DIBELS)	http://dibels.uoregon.edu
	Early Screening Project	http://www.nekesc.k12.ks.us/esp.html
	Kindergarten Curriculum-Based Measurement (K-CBM)	http://www.gosbr.net/screening
	Phonological Awareness Literacy Screening (PALS)	www.pals.virginia.edu
	Read Naturally	www.readnaturally.com/howto/orftable
Reading	AIMSWEB	www.aimsweb/com/measures/reading/sample.php
	Northwest Evaluation Association (NWEA)	www.nwea.org
	Harcourt	www.wirelessgeneration.com
	Pearson Prosper	www.pearsonncs.com
	Pearson Benchmark	www.pearsonschoolsystems.com
	Riverside Assess2Know	www.riverpub.com
	Developmental Reading Assessment	www.pearsonschool.com
	Benchmark Assessment Systems	www.tungstenlearning.com
	Learning Access!	www.vantagelearning.com
	CTB McGraw-Hill	www.ctn.com
	Renaissance Learning STAR Reading, Math, and Early Literacy	www.renlearn.com
Mathematics	AIMSWEB	www.aimsweb/com/measures/math/sample.php
	Northwest Evaluation Association (NWEA)	www.nwea.org
	Pearson Prosper	www.pearsonncs.com
	Pearson Benchmark	www.pearsonschoolsystems.com
	Riverside Assess2Know	www.riverpub.com
	Benchmark Assessment Systems	www.tungstenlearning.com
	Learning Access!	www.vantagelearning.com
Curriculum	Curriculum Based Measure	http://www.education.umn.edu/Pubs/ResearchWorks/CBM.html
		www.easycmb.com
		www.oswego.edu/~mcdougalkasp.org/tools
		www.jimwrightonline.com/php/chartdog_20/chartdog.php
		www/easy

* District Quarterly Assessments

* Common Formative (teacher made) Assessments

*Not meant as an endorsement of any of the screening instruments listed

EXHIBIT 4.9 Universal Assessment Form

Universal Assessment Form

F. Teacher:

G. School: Eagle Elementary School   Grade: _____   Date of Assessment: _____

I. (G) Proficient: _____   (Y) Close to Proficient: _____   (R) Significantly Below Proficiency _____

Students	Reading	Writing	Math	Behavior/Performance

An easy way to quickly see groups of students requiring intervention is to highlight in color

(G) Green = proficient; (Y) Yellow = close to proficient; and (R) Red or pink highlight = significantly below proficient.

EXHIBIT 4.10   Progress Monitoring Report

Initial date: _____

Name of Student: _____ Date of Birth: _____ Age: _____

Specify target or intensive group: _____
List names:

School: _____ District: _____ Grade: _____

City: _____ State: _____

Progress Monitor: _____ Position: _____

     1. What is the problem? (Assessment/Date):

     2. Which research-based intervention will be monitored (based on team analysis)?

     3. Which method(s) and frequency will be used to progress monitor?
     ☐ Assessment scores:_____ (Name/results/dates)
     ☐ Administrative walk-through/sweeps: _____ (Dates and times)
     ☐ Observations: _____ (Frequency/class/dates/time)
     ☐ Interviews: _____ (Name(s)
     ☐ Data Team/PLC:_____ (Dates results)

     Universal screening results (Fall) _____

     Universal Screening results (Winter) _____

     Universal Screening results (Spring) _____

     Behavior notes:

EXHIBIT 4.10 **Progress Monitoring Report** *(continued)*

Student/Group (continued) _____

Progress monitoring data:

Baseline   Intervention ————————————————————————————→

Baseline results:

Monitoring intervals: ☐ Daily ☐ Bi-weekly ☐ Weekly ☐ Bi monthly ☐ Monthly

Ref.#	Monitoring narrative (Date/Results):	Determine effectiveness or need for further change in intensity, time, or resources (date /results):

| EXHIBIT 4.11 | Template for Progress Monitoring Team Analysis |

Student(s):

Problem Statement:	
Strengths:	Inferences:
Challenge/Weakness:	Inferences:
Root cause:	

All Interventions must be provided with fidelity

Tier 1	Universal	Provide high quality scientifically research based instruction and differentiation of content, process or product in general education. This applies to all students based on their individual needs.
Tier 2	Target	General education instruction of Tier 1 plus specialized intervention that includes consideration of small group, specific minutes per day or week lasting approx 30 mins each session.
Tier 3	Intensive	Students that did not respond to Tier 2 interventions require intensive instruction that includes more frequency, duration and smaller groups sometimes 1:1.

References

Ainsworth, L. 2006. *Common Formative Assessments*. Thousand Oaks, CA: Corwin Press.

Applebaum, M. 2009. *The One Stop Guide to Implementing RTI: Academic and Behavioral Interventions, K–12*. Thousand Oaks, CA: Corwin Press/Sage.

Bender, W.N. 2009. *Beyond the RTI Pyramid: Solutions for the First Years of Implementation*. Bloomington, IN: Solution Tree Press.

Brown-Chidsey, R., L. Bronaugh, and K. McGraw. 2009. *RTI in the Classroom: Guidelines and Recipes for Success*. New York: Guilford Press.

Colorado State Department of Education (CDE). 2008. *Response to Intervention (RTI): A Practitioner's Guide to Implementation*. Denver: CDE.

Ehren, B.J., T.C. Ehren, and J.L. Proly. 2009. *Response to Intervention: An Action Guide for School Leaders*. Alexandria, VA: Education Research Service (ERS).

Fuchs, D., L.S. Fuchs, and S. Vaughn. 2008. *Response to Intervention: A Framework for Reading Educators*. Nashville, TN: National Research Center on Learning Disabilities.

Heacox, D. 2002. *Differentiating Instruction in the Regular Classroom: How to Reach and Teach All Learners, Grades 3–12*. St. Paul, MN: Free Spirit Publishing.

House, S.N., ed. 2004. *Learning Intervention Manual: Goals, Objectives, and Intervention Strategies*. Columbia, MO: Hawthorne Educational Services.

Howard, M. 2008. *Response to Intervention: Practical Strategies for Intervening with Students Before They Fall Too Far Behind in Reading (Grades 1–5)*. Bellevue, WA: Bureau of Education & Research.

lDonline.org., n.d. *Response to Intervention*. Accessed October 1, 2009.

Individuals with Disabilities Education Improvement Act (IDEIA). 2004. Washington, D.C.: U.S. Department of Education.

Jimerson, S.R., M.K. Burns, and A. VanDerHeyden. 2007. *Handbook of Response to Intervention: The Science and Practice of Assessment and Intervention*. New York: Springer Publications.

Kurns, S., and W.D. Tilly. 2008. "Response to Intervention Blueprints for Implementation: School Building Level." Alexandria, VA: National Association of State Directors of Special Education Council of Administrators of Special Education.

Marzano, R.J. 2007. *The Art and Science of Teaching: A Comprehensive Framework for Effective instruction*. Alexandria, VA: ASCD.

English Language Learners
and Data Teams

A PRACTICAL LENS

"Lively learning communities must be mindful and meaningful learning communities—interested in the children who come to school each day as well as attentive to results. They are places for celebration and commiseration as well as for constructing clear plans. They are informed by statistical evidence and by the wisdom of accumulated experience."

ANDREW HARGREAVES, 2010[*]

Mr. Juan Córdova helps teachers of English language learners (ELLs) by seeing the importance of Data Teams in meeting the needs of their leaders. His practical approach to disaggregation of data in subgroups helps us see the practical nature of deliberate instruction.

*Hargreaves, A., and D. Shirley, eds. 2009. *The Fourth Way: The Inspiring Future for Educational Change.* Thousand Oaks, CA. Corwin Press, p. 94.

CHAPTER 5

English Language Learners and Data Teams

JUAN CÓRDOVA

The Data Teams process—with its embedded teacher collaboration, focus on strength and obstacles, use of common data, and inherent teacher professional growth and development—can create the learning environment to assist all students—including English language learners—in making significant academic gains.

Marie Fuentes walked up the stairs slowly as she looked over her list of students for the upcoming year. As expected, she was going to be one of the two English language learner (ELL) inclusion teachers in fourth grade. When she volunteered for the job, she was excited. She had been an ELL student when she moved to the United States. She wanted to help the students the way that she had been helped. What she didn't expect was the number of ELL students she was going to have in her classroom. Twelve of her twenty-four kids were ELL students—more than she thought. She couldn't wait to talk to Jennifer to see what her class looked like.

Jennifer Sagendorph smiled as she looked at her class roll. This was the fifth year in a row that she would be an ELL inclusion teacher. It was a labor of love, and each year she had learned more and more about how to teach ELL students. Even though fourteen of her twenty-three kids were ELLs, she knew that she could reach them. She had done so in the past with increasing success. Her only concern was how she and Marie would work together as a Data Team. Jennifer had been in an ELL Data Team for the past four years, and each year, she had needed to teach the new ELL teacher about the process. She knew that the Data Teams process was effective, but she never felt that the ELL Data Teams fully reached their potential.

There was something missing—something she hadn't put her finger on yet. Maybe this year would be different.

Every fall, the situation above is repeated in schools across the United States. Teachers are given the "opportunity" to be an ELL teacher or an ELL inclusion teacher. Each year, teachers are asked to move ELL students from nonproficiency to proficiency. Each year, thousands of schools do not reach adequate yearly progress (AYP) because the ELL subgroup does not reach the level of proficiency required. ELL students, who by definition are nonproficient in English, are expected to become proficient quickly in order to meet state or federal goals. The pressure is immense.

The ELL Phenomenon

More than 50 million people in the United States speak a language other than English at home (U.S. Census Bureau, 2003). In keeping with that trend, the number of ELL students has exploded over the last fifteen years. From about two million ELL students in public schools during the 1993–1994 school year, to three million students in 1999–2000, to almost five million students in 2006, ELL students continue to be one of the fastest-growing segments within public schools (U.S. Department of Education, 2006). The exponential rise in the number of ELL students has led many schools to reexamine their ELL techniques and look for new ways to accelerate the acquisition of English language skills.

Exhibit 5.1 provides a visual representation of the growth of ELL students in public schools. The trend line (in solid black) shows that the ELL subgroup continues to grow, expanding by almost one million students in short four years. While numbers of ELL students are not available for the 2009–2010 school year, it is not unrealistic to think that the numbers could be close to six million students and growing.

The implementation of No Child Left Behind has also contributed heavily to the pursuit of new ways to accelerate learning for ELL students. Because No Child Left Behind requires schools to achieve proficiency for all students, schools have looked at their student achievement data in a more disaggregated fashion. ELL student achievement has lagged behind that of the majority group. Because the very definition of ELL is nonproficiency in English, schools must find ways to focus on ELL students and help them to raise their academic performance with a laser-like precision.

Data Teams: A Viable Solution

So we must ask the question, "If Data Teams have been shown to improve student performance in a school, can the use of Data Teams focused on ELL students

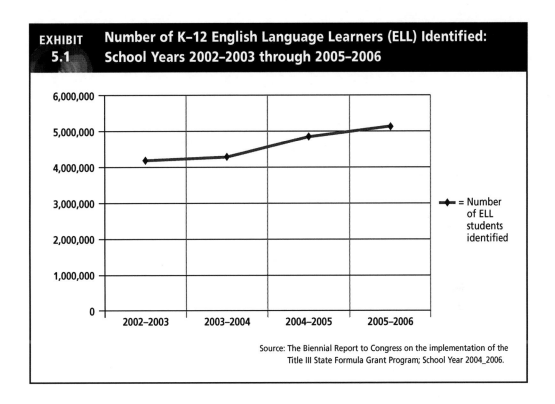

EXHIBIT 5.1 Number of K–12 English Language Learners (ELL) Identified: School Years 2002–2003 through 2005–2006

◆ = Number of ELL students identified

Source: The Biennial Report to Congress on the implementation of the Title III State Formula Grant Program; School Year 2004_2006.

produce similar results?" The Leadership and Learning Center has demonstrated in schools across the United States and beyond that the use of Data Teams, appropriately implemented, can be the engine for growth in student achievement. School districts from Virginia to California and from Michigan to Texas have all implemented the Data Teams process and have seen remarkable results. The Data Teams process—with its embedded teacher collaboration, focus on strength and obstacles, use of common data, and inherent teacher professional growth and development—can create the learning environment to assist all students—including ELL students—in making significant academic gains.

ELL Data Teams: Proficient Level

Jennifer and Marie sat together and looked at the data from the pre-test common formative assessment. "Main idea" and "supporting details" have always been a struggle at the beginning of the year, but if the kids didn't master this standard, they wouldn't be able to master the more challenging reading standards to come. As they looked at their data, Jennifer and Marie were not surprised. In Marie's class, eighteen of her twenty-four students did not reach the 80 percent mastery level and were nonproficient. Jennifer's class was only slightly better, with sixteen of her

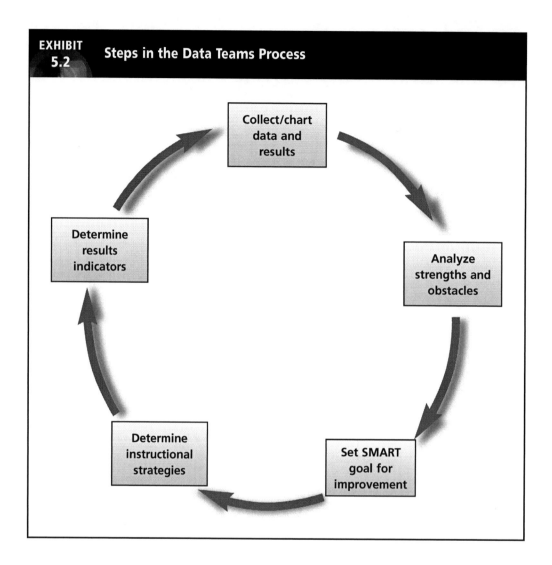

EXHIBIT 5.2   Steps in the Data Teams Process

Collect/chart data and results

Analyze strengths and obstacles

Set SMART goal for improvement

Determine instructional strategies

Determine results indicators

twenty-three students (69 percent) being nonproficient. Between the two of them, they had thirteen proficient students and thirty-four nonproficient students.

Jennifer pulled out the Data Teams training manual that she received during the training seminar from The Leadership and Learning Center. She wanted to review the process with Marie to make certain that they were both on the same page. She knew that each step was important and didn't want to forget any steps. Looking at Exhibit 5.2, she saw that she and Marie had already completed Step 1 of the process, collecting and charting the data and results.

If you look at the charted data in Exhibit 5.3, the overall levels of proficiency for a pre-test are not out of line for initial assessment on new material. It is not unreasonable to have low proficiency numbers prior to instruction. You haven't taught this material yet! Yet, there are students who *have* demonstrated overall

EXHIBIT 5.3	Sample Chart to Determine Initial Status of Students							
Name of Teacher	Number Tested	Number Proficient	Percent Proficient	Number Nonproficient	Percent Nonproficient	Names of students close to proficiency (60%–80%)	Names of students far to go (40%–60%)	Names of students in need of extensive support (< 40%)
Fuentes	24	6	25	18	75	Susan, Brittany, Selina, William, Jordon	**Maria, Isabella, Jose, Guillermo, Josefa, Catalina**	**Juan, Manuel, Luz, Esther, Hector, Alfredo**
Sagendorph	23	7	30.4	16	69.6	Malik, Cody, Grace, Joelle, Sean, Richard, Troy	**Pablo, Esteban, Jorge, Kimberly, Anna**	**Gil, Emmanuel, Samuel, Alexis**
TOTAL	47	13		34				

Note: Names of ELL students appear in **bold**.

mastery on this assessment. The Data Teams process can provide a systematic way of ascertaining the initial status of the students and therefore inform you on what your next steps should be.

However, reviewing overall proficiency is not using the Data Teams process to its fullest potential. *It is more informative to look at proficiency by individual standard.* By disaggregating the data further and charting out both classes by the standards evaluated via the common formative assessment, you can use the evidence provided to more effectively move to Step 2 of the Data Teams process and make more accurate inferences on areas of strengths and obstacles in learning. By making more precise inferences on strengths and obstacles, we have a more accurate perspective on what is needed for instruction. Using the Data Teams process provides us with the means of shaping our instruction based on specific needs of students rather than inoculating everyone in the class with the same instruction. In addition, by looking at the specific items on the assessments and seeing what patterns you can find, you can further shape instruction to the specific needs of your class. Students who have already mastered the skills can be provided with opportunities to go deeper with the standard, facilitating the enriched learning needed by the highfliers. For those who haven't mastered the standards, initial instruction can be further differentiated, and specific techniques can be applied to groups of students who are at different levels of understanding.

Exhibits 5.4 and 5.5 show proficiency by standard ("main idea" and "supporting details"). As you can see from the Exhibits 5.4 and 5.5, there are a number of students whose mastery or level of mastery has changed according to the standard. There are still no ELL students who have mastered "main idea," but there are some who have mastered "supporting details." In addition, there are some non-ELL students within the class who also have not mastered "main idea." Overall, the level of mastery for "main idea" is lower than the initial chart demonstrated.

The "supporting details" standard yields different results. Two students have mastered the standard. In addition, two students are close to mastering the standard, while the number of ELL students who are significantly away from mastery includes seven students. This is a dramatically different view of the data than was seen from the initial data in which the standards were combined. Using this more focused approach, you can infer that, overall, students had a greater

EXHIBIT 5.4	Chart Showing Proficiency by Standard ("Main Idea")							
Main Idea								
Name of Teacher	Number Tested	Number Proficient	Percent Proficient	Number Nonproficient	Percent Nonproficient	Names of students close to proficiency (60%–80%)	Names of students far to go (40%–60%)	Names of students in need of extensive support (< 40%)
Fuentes	24	5	25	19	75	Bill, Susan, Brittany, John	**Maria, Isabella, Jose,** Selina, William, Jordon	**Juan, Manuel, Luz, Esther, Hector, Alfredo, Guillermo, Josefa, Catalina**
Sagendorph	23	6	30.4	17	69.6	Malik, Cody, Grace, Joelle, Sean, Barbara	**Pablo, Esteban, Jorge, Kimberly, Anna,** Richard, Troy	**Gil, Emmanuel, Samuel, Alexis**
TOTAL	47	11		36				

Note: Names of ELL students appear in **bold**.

EXHIBIT 5.5	Chart Showing Proficiency by Standard ("Supporting Details")

Supporting Details

Name of Teacher	Number Tested	Number Proficient	Percent Proficient	Number Nonproficient	Percent Nonproficient	Names of students close to proficiency (60%–80%)	Names of students far to go (40%–60%)	Names of students in need of extensive support (< 40%)
Fuentes	24	9	37.5	15	62.5	Brittany, Selina, William, Jordon, **Josefa**	**Maria, Isabella, Jose, Guillermo** Hector, Alfredo	**Juan, Manuel, Luz, Esther,**
Sagendorph	23	11	47.8	12	52.1	Joelle, Sean, Richard, Troy, **Pablo**	**Jorge, Kimberly, Anna, Alexis**	**Gil, Emmanuel, Samuel**
TOTAL	47	20		27				

Note: Names of ELL students appear in **bold**.

command on the "supporting details" standard coming into class than on the "main idea" standard. ELL students across both classes demonstrated a much higher level of mastery in the "supporting details" standard.

An ELL Data Team whose students were at the proficient level would then move to the next steps of the Data Teams process by creating their SMART goals and determining the strategies to be used and then their results indicators. The remainder of the process would proceed as follows:

Marie and Jennifer sat down to determine what their SMART goals should be for their classes. They knew that their goal should be Specific, Measurable, Achievable, Relevant, and Timely. Jennifer and Marie both knew that the "main idea" was the key to their students becoming accomplished readers. They also knew that they would be teaching "main idea" and "supporting details" throughout the year because this was a priority standard. They decided to have a short-term goal for this teaching cycle and a long-term goal for the year. The short-term SMART goals were:

> The percentage of fourth-graders in the two ESL inclusion classes scoring proficient or higher in "main idea" will increase from 23.4 percent to 50 percent by the end of the unit as measured by the

post–common formative assessment administered at the end of the month.

And . . .

The percentage of fourth-graders in the two ESL inclusion classes scoring proficient or higher in "supporting details" will increase from 42.5 percent to 60 percent by the end of the unit as measured by the post–common formative assessment administered at the end of the month.

The long-term SMART goals reflected school-based goals. AYP was a fact of life at school, and this year's reading proficiency levels had to be at 72 percent proficiency. While there were other ways of achieving AYP, both Marie and Jennifer were confident that by using the Data Teams process and focusing on the specific needs of their students, they could meet AYP goals. Therefore, their year-end SMART goal is as follows:

The percentage of fourth-graders in the two ESL inclusion classes scoring proficient or higher in both "main idea" and "supporting details" will increase from 23.4 percent to 72 percent by the end of the year, as measured by the state assessment administered in late spring.

Moving to Step 4, Marie and Jennifer decided that they were going to use non-linguistic representations as a strategy for teaching "main idea" and "supporting details." One method that they decided upon was to provide students with non-linguistic representations in the form of pictures cut out of magazines. Using a variation of Think–Write–Round Robin, each group would look at a picture in the packet and think about either a detail (if working on "supporting details") or what the picture was about (if working on "main idea").

Finally, in Step 5, the results indicators would be stated in the form of "the student will be able to. . . ."

Using the Data Teams in this manner will result in student achievement gains in all students but neglects to use some specific information that may generate even greater gains for the ELL students; the ELL students' level of language acquisition.

ELL Data Teams: Advanced Level

Using the Data Teams process as stated above will provide Marie and Jennifer with a process to focus, in a laser-like manner, on individual students within their classes. By using data to group students by levels of nonproficiency, teachers can better focus their instruction and interventions based on what individual students need instead of teaching to the entire group without regard to need. This will move teachers from using one instructional strategy with the entire group to using multiple strategies that are specifically chosen and geared to the needs of delineated groups of students who have similar needs for improvement.

A teacher with ELL students can drill down further by not only delineating which students are ELL students but also by tracking which levels of language acquisition the students have reached. Students who are at Level 1 have significantly different needs than students who are at Level 3 or higher. The abilities of ELL students in English vary, as do their proficiencies in their native language. Therefore, the strategies to be used with students of varying levels of language acquisition should be different.

Delineating the language acquisition level next to each of the ELL students further provides teachers with information that can be used to determine what strategies would be most advantageous. Looking at Exhibits 5.6 and 5.7, you can immediately see a pattern. Students whose language acquisition levels were lowest

EXHIBIT 5.6	Chart Showing Language Acquisition Levels Next to Students' Names ("Main Idea" Standard)

					Main Idea			
Name of Teacher	Number Tested	Number Proficient	Percent Proficient	Number Nonproficient	Percent Nonproficient	Names of students close to proficiency (60%–80%)	Names of students far to go (40%–60%)	Names of students in need of extensive support (< 40%)
Fuentes	24	5	25	19	75	Bill, Susan, Brittany, John	Maria (L2), Isabella (L2), Jose (2), Selina, William, Jordon	Juan (L1), Manuel (L1), Luz (L1), Hector (L2), Alfredo (L2), Guillermo (L2), Josefa (L3), Catalina (L4)
Sagendorph	23	6	30.4	17	69.6	Malik, Cody, Grace, Joelle, Sean, Barbara	Pablo (L3), Esteban (L3), Jorge (L2), Kimberly (L2), Anna (L2), Richard, Troy	Gil (L1), Emmanuel (L1), Samuel (L1), Alexis (L2)
TOTAL	47	11		36				

Note: Names of ELL students appear in **bold**.

EXHIBIT 5.7	**Chart Showing Language Acquisition Levels Next to Students' Names ("Supporting Details" Standard)**

Supporting Details

Name of Teacher	Number Tested	Number Proficient	Percent Proficient	Number Nonproficient	Percent Nonproficient	Names of students close to proficiency (60%–80%)	Names of students far to go (40%–60%)	Names of students in need of extensive support (< 40%)
Fuentes	24	9	37.5	15	62.5	Brittany, Selina, William, Jordon, **Josefa (L3)**	**Maria (L2), Isabella (L2), Jose (2), Guillermo (L2), Hector (L2), Alfredo (L2)**	**Juan (L1), Manuel (L1), Luz (L1), Esther (L1)**
Sagendorph	23	11	47.8	12	52.1	Joelle, Sean, Richard, Troy, **Pablo (L3)**	**Jorge (L2), Kimberly (L2), Anna (L2), Alexis (L2)**	**Gil (L1), Emmanuel (L1), Samuel (L1)**
TOTAL	47	20		27				

Note: Names of ELL students appear in **bold**.

were the same students who struggled most with the standards that are being assessed. In other words, ELL students whose language acquisition skills were in the Level 1 and Level 2 categories were least likely to score well on the common formative assessment, while students who were at Level 3 or higher scored higher on the common formative assessment. Because we are still focusing on the initial, pre-assessment, knowing an ELL student's language acquisition level allows for instruction that is more in line with his or her specific needs. Having this information also provides the teacher with some idea of what the student is capable of in English and what types of actions the teacher should take in order to move the student forward. Differentiation by need is much easier with this additional information. Looking at Exhibits 5.8 through 5.12, you can see how each level of language acquisition is matched to specific student abilities and teacher behaviors.

Returning to Marie's and Jennifer's classes, these two teachers can now determine their strategies in the following fashion:

1. Provide initial instruction for the entire group in both "main idea" and "supporting details" using nonlinguistic representations; for example, using pictures and having students determine what the picture may be

EXHIBIT 5.8	Language Acquisition Level 1	
General Descriptor	**Students Can**	**Teacher Should**
Student moves from silent stage with no comprehension to physical responses with minimal comprehension. Student continues to one- or two-word responses with limited comprehension to speaking in simple sentences with comprehension of highly contextualized information.	• Respond nonverbally to respond in simple sentences • Respond in L1 • Respond physically • Sing and draw • Make connections with prior knowledge • Categorize objects and pictures • Use context to make meaning • Identify people, places and things • Repeat and recite • Reproduce what they hear • Label drawings and diagrams • Describe concrete things, events, places, and people • Explain simple academic concepts • Learn "big ideas" in content areas • Recognize and read basic vocabulary and write words and simple sentences • Associate sound and meaning • Role play • Listen and respond with greater comprehension • Compare and contrast	• Provide listening and speaking opportunities • Create a language-rich classroom • Create high context for shared reading • Use art, mime, and music • Use predictable, patterned books • Ask Yes/No, and Who? What? Where? questions • Have students label, manipulate and evaluate pictures and objects • Ask questions requiring responses of lists of words • Ask open-ended questions • Have students describe personal experiences • Use self-created books • Use props and realia during instruction • Assess prior knowledge and build background knowledge • Encourage active participation of listening, speaking, reading, and writing at the students' levels • Do informal assessments on an ongoing basis • Be patient

(Note: English learners are capable of higher-level thinking but are often unable to communicate their thoughts and ideas in spoken or written English.)

about. They use this activity to build better student comprehension of both the "main idea" and the "supporting details."

2. Create learning centers that are differentiated by how far away from mastery the students may be.

3. Provide specific scaffolding for the ELL students, taking into account their language acquisition level. Level 1 encourages students to respond

EXHIBIT 5.9 Language Acquisition Level 2

General Descriptor	Students Can	Teacher Should
Student moves from minimal comprehension and some proficiency in communicating simple ideas to comprehension of highly contextualized information. Student continues to speak in simple sentences with approximations. Reading and writing progress with scaffolding and support.	• Reproduce familiar phrases • Originate and speak in simple phrases • Speak with frequent errors in the patterns and structure of English • Make increased connections with prior knowledge • Use context to make meaning and increased connections • Simply describe people, places, and things along with more abstract concepts and ideas • Simply retell main events and the sequence of a story with some detail • Explain and describe simple academic concepts • Learn "big ideas" and details in content areas • Recognize and read basic vocabulary and write words and simple sentences • Listen and respond with greater comprehension	• Give more comprehensible input • Give students increased opportunities to produce academic and social language • Create a language-rich classroom • Create high context for shared reading • Use art, mime, and music • Ask Yes/No, and Who? What? Where? questions (literal responses) • Encourage expanded responses • Ask questions requiring simple comparisons, descriptions, and sequencing of events • Ask open-ended questions • Develop story frames • Provide increased practice of key grammatical structures in context • Have students describe personal experiences • Use self-created books • Use props and realia during instruction • Assess prior knowledge and build background knowledge • Encourage active participation of listening, speaking, reading, and writing at the students' levels • Do informal assessments on an ongoing basis. • Continue to monitor progress • Be patient

(Note: English learners are capable of higher-level thinking but are often unable to communicate their thoughts and ideas in spoken or written English.)

EXHIBIT 5.10	Language Acquisition Level 3	
General Descriptor	**Students Can**	**Teacher Should**
Student moves from comprehension of contextualized information and proficiency in communicating simple ideas to increased comprehension and communication skills. Student begins to speak in complex sentences with approximations. Reading and writing progress with scaffolding and support.	• Use context to make more meaning and increased connections to academic understanding • Engage in conversation and produce connected narrative • Interact with native speakers • Make errors with irregular patterns and structures in English • Read from a variety of genres with scaffolding from the teacher • Identify and describe main ideas and details • Simply summarize story or informational text • Make descriptions with increased details • Draw comparisons • Define new vocabulary	• Encourage students to describe personal and secondhand experiences • Provide explicit instruction in irregular patterns and structures in English and idiomatic expressions • Develop student study skills, such as making predictions and inferences • Explain text features as headings, charts, maps, and graphics • Provide opportunities to access technology • Engage students in directed reading–thinking activities • Use reciprocal teaching and learning to teach clarifying, questioning, summarizing, and predicting • Continue to develop vocabulary skills by providing comprehensible input • Develop cognitive skills through reading and writing • Ask how and why questions as well as open-ended, higher level thinking questions • Introduce explicit grammatical instruction • Do informal assessments on an ongoing basis. • Continue to monitor progress • Be patient

(Note: English learners are capable of higher-level thinking but are often unable to communicate their thoughts and ideas in spoken or written English.)

EXHIBIT 5.11	Language Acquisition Level 4	

General Descriptor	Students Can	Teacher Should
Student has good comprehension of information and proficiency to communicate well using both social and academic language. Students have an adequate vocabulary to achieve academically. Students are approaching grade level in reading and writing.	• Make fewer errors with irregular patterns and structures in English • Read from a variety of genres with little scaffolding from the teacher • Identify and describe complex main ideas with details • Summarize a story or informational text • Give opinions and reasons for their opinions C• an summarize, draw comparisons and contrasts, and justify views and behaviors • Demonstrate both social and academic understanding of English • Demonstrate the ability to use higher-order language, synthesize, analyze, and evaluate • Persuade and debate with preparation • Engage in extended conversations and produce complex sequential narrative • Develop listening, speaking, reading. and writing skills with increased comprehension	• Structure group discussions • Provide opportunities for readers' theater and literature circles • Provide for a variety of realistic writing opportunities • Guide use of reference materials and technology • Provide opportunities for reading a variety of genres • Publish student writing • Focus on academic language and vocabulary • Ask questions to provide students with opportunities to synthesize, analyze, and evaluate in oral and written communication • Expand explicit grammatical instruction • Do informal assessments on an ongoing basis • Continue to monitor progress • Be patient

(Note: English learners are capable of higher-level thinking but are often unable to communicate their thoughts and ideas in spoken or written English.)

physically or by drawing their answers, while Level 3 gives students opportunities to receive explicit work and practice in deriving the "main idea" and "supporting details."

4. Use cooperative learning opportunities for students to work together, thus building on the strength of the group.

All of the listed strategies are ideas that could be generated during Step 4 of the Data Teams process. The important points are that there should be an active

EXHIBIT 5.12	Language Acquisition Level 5	
General Descriptor	**Students Can**	**Teacher Should**
Student has very good comprehension of information and near-native proficiency to communicate using both social and academic language. Students have an expanded vocabulary to achieve academically. Students at or above grade level in reading and writing.	• Make few errors with irregular patterns and structures in English • Read from a variety of genres with little to no scaffolding from the teacher • Comprehend and generate discussions and presentations in social and academic settings • Have developed fluency with a wide range of topics • Read and comprehend grade-level texts • Organize and generate written compositions based on purpose, audience, and subject matter • Have a sense of their own voice • Respond to and use figurative language and idiomatic expressions appropriately • Prepare and deliver presentations and reports across grade-level content areas that use a variety of sources and that include purpose, point of view, transitions, and conclusions	• Continue explicit grammatical instruction • Encourage students to lead group discussions and teach • Provide opportunities for student-generated presentations • Provide for a variety of realistic writing opportunities in a variety of genres • Encourage independent use of reference materials and technology • Continue to publish student works • Provide increased opportunities for students to develop higher-order thinking skills • Do informal assessments on an ongoing basis. • Continue to monitor progress • Be patient

(Note: English learners are capable of higher-level thinking but are often unable to communicate their thoughts and ideas in spoken or written English.)

discussion about the ELL students within the Data Teams process, and strategies should be selected that meet students' language acquisition level. Using strategies that ignore what a child is capable of doing would be akin to using strategies that require sight for a student who is blind. It is not something that any teacher would do, yet it frequently can happen to ELL students.

ELL Data Teams: Exemplary Level

Gearing instruction to the fit the needs of ELL students is critical for success. ELL strategies are effective in providing an environment that is conducive for language acquisition. But not all ELL students are the same. There are various levels of language acquisition. These levels (refer to Exhibits 5.8 through 5.12) provide teachers with a road map for instruction. Using these levels of language acquisition is similar to using an individual education plan or a 504 plan. Looking at what students can do and what teachers should do promotes increased English language ability.

Using the Data Teams process within an ELL class will lead to a more focused instructional plan. Let's return to Marie's and Jennifer's classes and see how this would work.

Jennifer sat down and reflected that she should have been cautious about what she wished for. The principal had finally permitted her and Marie to carve out a separate time for ELL instruction. So now, the ELL students were going to get specific instruction in the forms and structures of the English language instead of just working on reading comprehension skills. While the principal insisted on continuing with the common formative assessments used by the remainder of the

---

EXHIBIT 5.13   **National Standard from Teachers of English to Speakers of Other Languages**

Goal 2, Standard 2
To use English to achieve academically in all content areas: Students will use English to obtain, process, construct, and provide subject matter information in spoken and written form

Descriptors
- Comparing and contrasting information
- Persuading, arguing, negotiating, evaluating, and justifying
- Listening to, speaking, reading, and writing about subject matter information
- Gathering information orally and in writing
- Retelling information
- Selecting, connecting, and explaining information
- Analyzing, synthesizing, and inferring from information
- Responding to the work of peers and others
- Representing information visually and interpreting information presented visually
- Hypothesizing and predicting
- Formulating and asking questions
- Understanding and producing technical vocabulary and text features according to content area
- Demonstrating knowledge through application in a variety of contexts

school, she did allow for thirty minutes a day of ELL instruction and the use of additional assessments for ELL students. This was going to be more work, but Jennifer believed that this was the proper way to go. Thankfully, Marie agreed.

They looked at the national ELL standards and agreed to use those as the standards they would teach within the ELL block. The next steps would be to create assessments to ascertain growth and adapt the Data Teams process to inform their instruction and remediation.

It is imperative that, at the very least, Level 1 through Level 2 students be provided with an ELL block that specifically focuses on the forms and structures of English. It is also important that the Data Teams process be used as a means of informing instruction. Using the national standard from Teachers of English to Speakers of Other Languages (Exhibit 5.13), you can see how this would look.

This standard basically states that students will use English to learn. However, demonstrating this ability would have to look differently at each level. Focusing on Levels 1 and 2, you can envision an assessment that has the students comparing and contrasting information.

Level 1 students could use a Venn diagram or a graphic organizer to allow them to place pictures in the various places, demonstrating in a nonverbal fashion the similarities and differences between the pictures. By using this nonverbal means of assessing comparison and contrast, you can ascertain whether the ELL student has mastered the portion of the standard being assessed and is being inhibited by an inability to express it in English, or whether the student hasn't mastered that portion of the standard. This is a critical difference. As students acquire an increasingly greater ability in English, they will make the transference to expressing themselves linguistically. This inability should not preclude them from being able to learn the standards.

The Data Teams process would then collect and chart the data, allowing the teacher to then make judgments and inferences on the level of mastery of the students being assessed. This would, in turn, provide the teacher with the information necessary to adapt the instruction. If this was a pre-test, the teacher would shape instruction according to the data; if it was a post-test, the teacher would create remediation and/or enrichment based on the data. Regardless of the place on the teaching–learning cycle, teachers—by using the Data Teams process—can better create instruction tailored for their students. By keeping in mind the language acquisition levels of students, teachers can design the assessments with the students' specific abilities in mind. Central to making any and all of these adjustments is the Data Teams process. The five steps of the Data Teams process inform instruction.

Professional Growth and Development

So far, our discussion has focused on the Data Teams process, the collecting and charting of data, and the selection of instructional strategies. Another element of the Data Teams process that has a direct impact on ELL students is the collaboration and inherent professional growth and development that come from this collaboration. Using our example of Marie and Jennifer, Jennifer has taught ELL students for four years. Her success implies that, during this time, she has acquired a variety of skills and techniques that can be shared with Marie. In addition, Marie comes with her own set of knowledge and skills. Those experiences can also be added to the collective wisdom of the Data Team.

The Data Teams process creates that opportunity throughout the five steps. Each step requires discussion and collaboration. Each step illuminates whether all members of the process are equally skilled with the process or with the strategies that are discussed. If a strategy that is being discussed is one that a member of the Data Team group feels uncertain about, the Data Teams process provides the structure for the professional learning to occur. Instead of each individual within the group forging on his or her own, the power of the collective wisdom of the group is harnessed—in this case, for the benefit of the ELL students. Language acquisition is a difficult and time-intensive process. Sharing of ideas and techniques can only benefit the students. The Data Teams process permits the group to move from a series of independent fiefdoms connected by a common parking lot to a collective wisdom for the students—a much better proposition.

Data Teams: Providing the Tools for ELL Success

While the examples used in this chapter have all been from elementary schools, the principles discussed can also be used in secondary schools. Using the Data Teams process can be done either vertically (within specific disciplines) or horizontally (across a specific grade level and thus crossing disciplines). The five-step process can be used at the proficient level, at the advanced level, at the exemplary level, or, at times, at all three levels within a school. The critical piece is that the process should be used to improve student achievement, especially for ELL students. By focusing specifically on the language acquisition levels of students, the Data Teams process can create instruction that specifically focuses on ELL students' explicit needs. By harnessing the power of the collective wisdom of the group working with ELL students, knowledge and wisdom can be shared and students will again benefit.

Our ELL population needs smarter—not harder—work. With the exponential growth of the group, ELL students are rapidly becoming students whom all schools will have as part of their student body instead of students who are found only in large school districts in California, Texas, Florida, and New York. No Child Left Behind requires schools and systems to meet the needs of all students, regardless of how they come to us. The Data Teams process can provide teachers and schools with the tools necessary to make it happen.

References

No Child Left Behind. PL–107–10. Available at http://www2.ed.gov/policy.elsec/leg/esea02/index.html.

Teachers of English to Speakers of Other Languages. "ESL Standards for Pre-K–12 Students." Available at http://www.tesol.org/s_tesol/sec_document.asp?CID=113&DID-315.

U.S. Census Bureau. 2003. *USA Quickfacts.* Available at http://quickfacts.census.gov.qfd/states/00000.html. Accessed April 22, 2010.

U.S. Department of Education. 2006. "The Biennial Data Report to Congress on the Implementation of the Title III State Formula Grant Program School Year 2004–2006." Available at http://www.ncela.gwu.edu/files/uploads/3/Biennial_Report_0406.pdf.

Twenty-First Century Schooling and Data Teams

A PRACTICAL LENS

> *"Changing our mental models about what we teach, how we teach it, and how we assess students' learning growth will take some getting used to. Such changes require open-mindedness, flexibility, patience, and courage."*
>
> HAYES–JACOBS, 2010*

Mr. Ainsley Rose challenges our beliefs in education and encourages us to radically and creatively think about how we view teaching and learning in the twenty-first century.

*Hayes–Jacobs, H. 2010. *Curriculum 21: Essential Education for a Changing World.* Alexandria, VA: ASCD, p. 211.

CHAPTER 6

Twenty-First Century Schooling and Data Teams

AINSLEY ROSE

We must model what we expect our students to engage in.
To suggest that students alone will derive benefit from
a twenty-first century curriculum is negating the notion
that we all need to be lifelong learners.
The Data Teams process allows teachers to model the
very behaviors that we want students to acquire and use.

The movie *Avatar*, the 2010 rage in movie land, depicts life in a land called Pandora circa 2154. (Interestingly, the word "avatar" is defined as an "incarnate divine teacher" [MacBook Pro Dictionary, 2010].) Pandora is fraught with all of the trials and tribulations of our present world. The plot revolves around the quest for a special mineral called unobtanium (how appropriate) and the indigenous people who inhabit Pandora and live in harmony with nature. The historical tension between good and evil is played out in this fictional account with the same perspective we currently depict the hero and villain. Little has changed, even in our prediction and imagination of a future world in this, the twenty-first century.

This vignette points out that even our creative future scenarios remain entrapped by our current level of thinking. If, in the area of increased creative freedom, we continue only to demonstrate futuristic thoughts based on current, often limited imagination, what is the likelihood that our school systems will be any different than present arcane models? Indeed, our schools have not changed since the dawn of the industrial revolution—the very era that spawned our current model of schooling, organizational patterns of education, assessment, and beliefs about what constitutes student success.

Therefore, if *Avatar* and its multimillion-dollar budget, creative effects, technological innovations, creative and imaginative writers, and high-priced actors are not able to move beyond old paradigms of good and evil, conqueror and vanquished, can we possibly think of schools with curricula, systems, practices, and procedures as being different? Or, will we merely replicate current practices—save for the possible addition of whiteboards, computers in sterile lab arrays replete with video-conferencing units—and say that we now have twenty-first century schools and curricula? Surely, there is more to it than that.

We are left with several intriguing questions, such as:

- What twenty-first century skills will schools be asked to teach and then be held accountable for?

- Will this require a reengineering of our present structure or model for schooling?

- What new skills will teachers need to acquire in order to be effective in the classroom, if, indeed, there is such a thing as a classroom?

- How can we expect teachers to assess, evaluate, and judge student progress in these new skills and subjects?

You may well have other questions that could and should be the focus of future writings.

This chapter considers some of the questions that teams of teachers will face in the future as educational systems and other influential public bodies call for an increased emphasis on what we have come to know as "twenty-first century skills." In light of current effective practices such as the Data Teams process, now in vogue in many successful schools, what might we have to consider to either preserve what makes such a process effective, or how will we need to amend current procedures?

Twenty-First Century Skills: What Are They?

What these skills are remains largely undefined, although there are certainly many suggestions about what these skills should or could be. Strangely, though, it appears that they resemble skills that schools have been trying unsuccessfully to teach to the legions of students for a long, long time.

What is interesting about our prediction of what the future holds for students presently in the system and for those to come is that we really don't know with any certainty what the future really does hold for all of us, let alone what the educational system might look like. As Davies and Ellison (1997) illustrate in *School Leadership for the 21st Century*, the notion of the "extended present" suggests that families can trace backward using oral history provided by parents and grandparents of events of fifty or eighty years ago; however, they are not as adept at surmising some of the trends that will shape the future even in ten to fifteen years (p. 12). The Partnership for 21st Century Skills (2010) makes a similar contention when it says, "Education, after all, is the attempt to convey from one generation to the next the skills, values, and knowledge that are needed for successful life" (p. 1). So, then, how can schools and school systems, let alone the communities that these schools serve, hope to predict what we should be preparing our students for with any degree of certainty while ensuring the transference of these former skills, values, and knowledge? You may well recall in the early 1960s the universal call to create programs in schools to ready that generation of students for increased leisure time, given the advent of shorter work weeks and technological innovations that would have us all with nothing to do. Did this ever materialize? I think not.

All we can really say is that it will be different than what it is now. When a student enters the school system at age five in 2010, he or she will hope to graduate at some point in the year 2023, given our present rules of engagement in the school system. Can we truly expect that there are enough of us with the clairvoyance and assurance to suggest that we know what is needed to prepare this student for the year 2023? To quote Davies and Ellison (1997):

> "Incremental change may not be sufficient for dealing with the fundamental shifts in technology and pattern of work. What is probably needed is a much more radical and fundamental rethink of the nature of society, education and the role of the school" (p. 14).

Many educators and much literature suggest that the new curriculum be centered on our preoccupation with technology and its use in future classrooms. This is, at best, a narrow and limited view of what schools need to engage future students in if we are to truly invoke new thinking about what a twenty-first century curriculum is really all about. While technology, in the broadest sense, is a critical element of present life, we need to remember that computers in particular are not a new phenomenon. However, the ubiquity, speed of connectivity, and social behavior that their use has spawned are provoking us not to ignore their impact. Our need, therefore, to prepare our present generations to deal with the fallout from this modern revolution is akin to that illustrated by the development of the Gutenberg printing press (Kamm, Rshaid, and Rose, 2010).

Based on the mountain of literature that is now available about twenty-first century skills, we can ascertain three distinctive issues that will shape the conversations for schools and school systems around the world:

1. There is no consensus as to what twenty-first century skills are or should be. There is no shortage of ideas but there is little agreement.

2. Whether or not students are demonstrating (through assessment methods) these twenty-first century skills will remain a challenge of the highest order, particularly when we have not been successful in finding effective methods in the past with respect to the curriculum and evaluation methods.

3. How can we, with any degree of assurance, predict what future skills should be when we have not been able to do so for the past millennium? This might explain why school systems and those who toil earnestly in them are the subject of ridicule and vitriol when the nation fares unfavorably in the myriad of international tests that rank order students and, by implication, their countries.

Now let's examine what some of the "experts" proclaim to be the curriculum of the next generation of schools and what twenty-first century skills will be taught in them.

Heidi Hayes Jacobs (2010) of curriculum mapping fame hints at her version of what needs to be addressed if we are to make the curriculum appropriate to the new order of schooling. She states, "We need to overhaul, update, and inject life in to our curriculum and dramatically alter the format of what schools look like to match the time in which we live" (p. 3).

The Partnership for 21st Century Skills (2010) outlines its clarion call for the present curriculum to be augmented by the following themes:

- Global awareness
- Financial, economic, business, and entrepreneurial literacy
- Civic literacy
- Health literacy
- Environmental literacy

Other authors add versions of curricular expectations that appear neither innovative nor different than what schools have been trying to deliver without much success over the last century. Nevertheless, let us not dismiss these suggestions too hastily, because I believe that an examination of all of the suggestions might just reveal a kernel of consensus.

My preference comes from the writing of Ian Jukes (2009a), who outlines an interesting list recognizing the importance of retaining skills that will remain crucial even in the twenty-first century while expanding our thinking about how we might need to emphasize those skills using new filters.

1. Obsolete skills: May still be practiced for nostalgia but have been replaced

by other mainstream skills (e.g., sharpening swords, operating an elevator, delivering milk).

2. Traditional skills of decreased emphasis: Handwriting, hand accounting, the Dewey decimal system; not a necessity, but they continue to help cultivate mental processes.

3. Traditional literacy skills: Reading, writing, numeracy, research, traditional communication, and social skills. These are fundamental practices for transmitting culture to new generations and are still essential in the twenty-first century.

4. Traditional skills of increased emphasis: In our new digital age, this refers to the skills of information processing, critical thinking, problem solving, technology comprehension, and graphical communication.

5. New, or twenty-first century skills: These have emerged as technology has appeared. They are unique to our present digital generation. They include social networking and online communications (p. 15).

The Fluency Project (2010), with its mission to transform learning and schools, cites the following as the principles that shape the work of their organization:

> The 21st Century Fluency Project is a collaborative initiative that was created to develop exceptional educational resources to assist in transforming learning to be relevant to life in the 21st century. Our mission is simple—to instill awareness of the importance of the change that is happening today, to help educators understand the need to "catch up" to today's students by re-evaluating current instructional and assessment methods, and to provide guidance in how to make change a beneficial thing for both student and teacher (http://21stcenturyfluency.com/about.cfm).

Linda Darling–Hammond et al. (2008), an educational icon in the United States, weighs in with her rendition of twenty-first century skills:

- The capacity to design and manage one's own work
- Communicate effectively and collaborate with others
- Research ideas
- Collect, synthesize, and analyze information
- Develop new products
- Apply many bodies of knowledge to novel problems that arise

You can, on any given day, pull up lists of twenty-first century skills just by searching any educational Web site and viewing the various ideas about what schools should be teaching students, until the next millennium arrives. However, little mention is made of other aspects of human skills that we need to reinvigorate in our students. What of the human dimensions of compassion for your fellow man, morals, and ethical values of human beings, many of which have been eroded (Davies, 1997)?

What Should an Assessment of Twenty-First Century Skills Look Like?

The model of Professional Learning Communities (PLCs) made popular by Dufour and Eaker (1998) ask schools to consider four questions in order to guide the work of schools.

1. What do we want our students to learn?

2. How will we know they have learned?

3. What will we do when they don't?

4. What will we do when they already know it?

These four questions can serve as the backdrop as we attempt to answer the challenge of assessment of twenty-first century skills. Of particular note is that, whatever set of skills we can agree on as those that are most representative of what the new curriculum will look like, we are immediately faced with the consideration that some of these skills will be very hard to measure with conventional means. Just take the suggestions of Heidi Hayes Jacobs (2010) as one example, and ask yourself how you might go about determining the level of competency attainment of civic, environmental, or health literacy that she suggests should be key elements in this new curriculum? Will paper-and-pencil, selected-choice tests suffice to get at these new skills, or would constructed-response be more appropriate in this case? What if it is found that neither method reveals the true nature of the learner? Reeves (2009b) is more assertive in his outlook when he suggests, ". . . it is not possible to reconcile the demands of the twenty-first century with the reality of the traditional testing environment. Consider the contrast between what is expected of students and how we test them" (p. 3). Later he writes:

> . . . assessments that focus exclusively on what students know and do are worse than incomplete; omission of the other essential elements of the framework send the clear message to teachers that, in the parlance of the classroom, twenty-first century skills don't count. Without a combination of critical thinking, problem solving, effective teamwork, and creativity, learning remains stagnant, more useful for passing a test than solving a real-world challenge (p. 8).

There is some hope, however, as outlined in a report titled "Measuring Skills for the 21st Century" (2010) that purports that new models of assessment are now available that are able to measure both basic skills as well as more advanced skills that twenty-first century curricula will require.

How Will Teachers Learn to Adjust Their Teaching for Twenty-First Century Skills?

How can we expect that teachers are going to be able to encourage collaboration, creative thinking, examination of real-world issues, teamwork, and effective global graphical communication, among other skills, and then be expected to assess them using the only methods they presently know how to apply? Heidi Hayes Jacobs (2010) points out that, "as educators we need to become strategic learners ourselves by deliberately expanding our perspective and updating our approaches" (p. 7).

Costa and Kallick (1995) present a compelling description of the purpose of assessment when they write:

> We must constantly remind ourselves that the ultimate purpose of assessment is to create autonomous students who are self-analyzing, self-evaluating, self-referencing, self-renewing, and self-motivating. This requires that students develop internal feedback spirals as a means of setting goals, planning actions, gathering data about their actions, reflecting on their own values, and altering their behaviors and values accordingly (p. 117).

Will the new generation of digital natives (Tapscott, 2009) be expected to do likewise? Furthermore, what new skills will teachers need in order to create an appropriate environment for students to assume these responsibilities? The challenge, however, is that the more we rely on such methods, the greater the likelihood that the results will be reliable (Silva, 2010). While teachers maybe able to assess more effectively with greater depth and variety that reflect real-world applications, the level of subjectivity or inter-rater reliability increases exponentially. What can we do to encourage these new methods and still develop a level of professionalism, validity, and reliability—the cornerstones of effective assessment?

Clearly, one approach, in use in effective schools, occurs where teachers engage in professional behaviors by examining the evidence of student learning obtained through common formative classroom assessments. This approach has become known as the Data Teams process.

How the Data Teams Process Can Help
to Bridge the Gap from Learning to Teaching
in the Twenty-First Century Skills Context

By definition, a Data Team examines the evidence of student learning derived from common formative assessments, which are then used to inform future instruction. The concept of using results to inform instruction is an often-heard phrase suggesting that teachers understand that the assessments to which they subject students are used to make adjustments in the instructional process. But what does that really mean in practical terms in the classroom? On their own, teachers will find it more difficult to analyze the results of their assessments in order to make instructional decisions without having the wisdom of their colleagues to challenge their conclusions.

The four questions that shape the work of PLCs (outlined earlier) require evidence to determine the next steps—evidence that is derived mostly from common formative assessments. As we know from the prevailing research (Black and Wiliam, 1998; Hattie, 1992; Sadler, 1998), common formative assessment rivals one-on-one tutoring in terms of improving student achievement. By definition, common formative assessment requires the participation of colleagues in a collaborative process to plan, develop, administer, execute, and revise on the basis of the results obtained by teachers from their students.

Done alone, a teacher may not arrive at the appropriate conclusion about what to do next. The Data Teams process is a structured, proven approach that helps teachers analyze assessment results to specifically identify areas of student needs. It also serves to reduce teacher isolation—a common challenge in our schools and classrooms. Because learning is best achieved through a social, collaborative approach, surely that approach supports the learning of teachers in identifying the appropriate instructional strategies, skills, and tactics that best serve to increase student learning and achievement.

The decisions that we make on a daily basis about student acquisition of learning outcomes are part of an integrated, holistic system centered on student learning. The focus must be on what to teach, how to teach it, how to assess it, and how to be confident that these strategies are working for you and for your students. Douglas Reeves, founder of The Leadership and Learning Center in Englewood, Colorado, often reminds us that these decisions must be based on what the "preponderance of evidence" suggests are best for our students and the next steps in their learning journey. Any process that builds on the collective wisdom of the professionals in a school is surely more certain to bring a positive benefit, assuming that the process is followed and monitored to ensure fidelity.

The five-step process of a Data Team, as outlined by The Leadership and Learning Center, is specifically designed to accomplish this task and achieve a positive conclusion, especially if the participants align this work with other professional practices that research has shown produces gains in student achievement. Stephen White (2005) says in his early work *Beyond the Numbers*, "Data teams adhere to continuous improvement cycles, examine patterns and trends, and establish specific time lines, roles, and responsibilities to facilitate analysis that results in action" (p.18).

The five steps referred to are:

1. Collect and chart data.

2. Analyze strengths and obstacles.

3. Establish SMART goals: Set, review, and revise them.

4. Select instructional strategies.

5. Determine results indicators.

Done well, consistently, collaboratively, and supported by the principal of the school, teams of teachers will also achieve one of Rick Stiggins's (2004) favorite principles of assessment for learning—to increase the assessment literacy of the teachers in those schools.

The Data Teams process, while not a "silver bullet," is one process that, if combined with other research-proven, school-based strategies, will certainly lead to improved student achievement and greater learning gains for all of our students, including some of the hardest to engage.

Further Impact of Using Data Teams with This Area of Focus

The very nature of the clarion call to conceive of ways to educate children in new, more alternative ways that take into account the skills that are being referred to as "twenty-first century" would suggest that our present structure and process of Data Teams would need to evolve to reflect this new emphasis on skills currently lacking in most schools and school systems. For example, creative thinking is one of the cornerstones of what the experts refer to as "new" skills that schools should teach. What methods will have to be devised to gather evidence that students are expressing creativity? How that is manifested in what students are expected to produce will remain an interesting challenge when states and provinces push ahead with standardized, global student tests that will be held at the same time, on the same day, and at the same hour. A creative approach to assessment and evaluation, don't you think? What data might arise from such testing schemes that teachers will then be able to collaboratively examine in their Data Teams structure to make sensible decisions about what next to teach next and how to go about doing that with any degree of fidelity? This does not even consider practical applications of this new approach that is yet to be defined and modeled in the classrooms of a yet-to-be-seen twenty-first century school or classroom.

As Ian Jukes (2009a) points out in the excerpt from one of his many articles on the digital revolution:

> How can we reconcile these new developments with current instructional practices, particularly in a climate of standards and accountability driven by high-stakes testing for all? What strategies can we use to appeal to the learning preferences and communication needs of digital learners while at the same time honoring our traditional assumptions and practices related to teaching, learning and assessment (p.1)?

To emphasize the essence of this point, read the following from Davies and Ellison (1997), who support the aforementioned when they say: "So while technology dominates the world economy, the school curriculum should place great emphasis on the human effects of this revolution so that students become reactive, and moral shapers of events rather than passive spectators" (p. 172).

The Importance of Collaboration and Modeling Twenty-First Century Behaviors and Skills

This chapter began with a less-than-optimistic interpretation of the film *Avatar* and what might be a new vision of our future world, if only in our imagination. It raised the question of whether the educational system will fall victim to the same fate and merely appear to create a different system. Or, will it be courageous and actually alter how teaching and learning are delivered to current and future students? There are indeed hopeful views that this is possible. Heidi Hayes Jacobs (2010) puts it best when she says: "The way to modernize our work is not to use the computer instead of a typewriter and call it innovative. It is to replace existing practices. I believe the practical route is to start with assessments, then work on revising content and skills" (p. 18).

If, as she suggests, we need to begin with assessments, and given the dire warnings of Reeves (2009a) mentioned earlier, we have much work to do. Mere tinkering will not suffice. We need to understand that, because teachers hold the greatest hope for change as they modify their instructional strategies, school principals must create opportunities that permit teachers to function in collaborative structures, focused on examining student results arising from assessments that are substantially different than what students presently experience. We must ensure that such opportunities become the norm rather than the exception. We must model what we expect our students to engage in. To suggest that students alone will derive benefit from a twenty-first century curriculum is negating the notion that we all need to be lifelong learners. The Data Teams process allows teachers to model the very behaviors that we want students to acquire and use. Once again, Ian Jukes (2009a) provides some further insight: "The current educational system is trying to fit square-peg students into round-hole schools, and using standardized tests to measure increasingly nonstandardized brains. We need to consider how to restructure the classroom experience; the way we teach, the way students learn, and how that learning is assessed" (p. 1).

The precious metal in *Avatar* was "unobtanium." Let us not continue to have to search metaphorically for this elusive substance in our school systems.

References

Black, P., and D. Wiliam. 1998. "Inside the Black Box: Raising Standards Through Classroom Assessment." *Phi Delta Kappan,* vol. 80, no. 2, pp. 139–148.

Costa, A.L., and B. Kallick, eds. 1995. *Assessment in the Learning Organization: Shifting the Paradigm.* Alexandria, VA: ASCD.

Daly, James. November 14, 2009. "A Teacher's Thoughts: Learning and Science in the 21st Century." *Looking Beyond the Easy Measurements.* Available at http://ateachersthoughts.com/. Accessed February 3, 2010.

Darling–Hammond, L., et al. 2008. *Powerful Learning: What We Know About Teaching for Understanding.* San Francisco: Jossey–Bass.

Datnow, A., V. Park, and B. Kennedy. 2008. *Acting on Data: How Urban High Schools Use Data to Improve Instruction.* Center on Educational Governance, USC Rossier School of Education: New Schools Venture Fund.

Davies, B., and L. Ellison. 1997. *School Leadership for the 21st Century: A Competency and Knowledge Approach.* London and New York: Routledge.

DuFour, R., and R. Eaker. 1998. *Professional Learning Communities at Work: Best Practices for Enhancing Student Achievement.* Bloomington, IN: Solution Tree.

Friedman. T.L. 2006. *The World is Flat: A Brief History of the Twenty-First Century.* New York: Farrar, Straus and Giroux.

Future of Learning. Available at http://www.futureofed.org/learningagent/Learning-Fitness-Instructor.aspx. Accessed February 22, 2010.

Hargreaves, A., and D. Shirley. 2009. *The Fourth Way: The Inspiring Future for Educational Change.* Thousand Oaks, CA: Corwin.

Hattie, J.A. 1992. "Measuring the Effects of Schooling." *Australian Journal of Education,* vol. 36, no. 1, pp. 5–13.

http://www.edutopia.org/future-school. Accessed February 12, 2010.

http://www.nytimes.com/2010/02/12/education/12bus.html?partner=rss&emc=rss. Accessed February 13, 2010.

Jacobs, H.H., ed. 2010. *Curriculum 21: Essential Education for a Changing World.* Alexandria, VA: ASCD.

Jukes, I. 2009a. *Living on the Future Edge.* Available at www.thecommittedsardine.com. Accessed February 8, 2010.

———. 2009b. *Understanding The Digital Generation 15.* Available at www.thecommittedsardine.com. Accessed February 8, 2010.

Kamm. C., G. Rshaid, and A. Rose. 2010 (forthcoming). *Transforming Education in the Digital Age (or 21st Century).* 21st Century Institute Proposal (in draft). Englewood, CO: The Leadership and Learning Center.

Mac Dictionary, Online. 2010.

Returning to Learning in an Age of Assessment: Introducing the Rationale of the Collegiate Learning Assessment. August 18, 2009. Available at http://www.collegiatelearningassessment.org/files/ReturningToLearning.pdf. Accessed February 21, 2010.

Silva, E. 2010. "Measuring Skills for the 21st Century." Washington, D.C.: Education Sector Reports. Available at http://www.educationsector.org/usr_doc/MeasuringSkills.pdf.

Pickett, N., and B. Dodge. 2001. "Rubrics for Web Lessons." Available at http://edweb.sdsu.edu/webquest/rubrics/weblessons.htm.

Reeves, D. 2009a. "A New Framework for Assessing 21st Century Skills." PDF presentation at The Leadership and Learning Center retreat, Denver, CO, November 2009.

———. 2009b. "Assessing 21st Century Skills: Principles and Paradoxes." PDF presentation at The Leadership and Learning Center retreat, Denver, CO, November 2009.

Sadler, D.R. March 1998. "Formative Assessment: Revisiting the Territory." *Assessment in Education,* vol. 5, no. 1, pp. 77–84.

Stiggins, R.J., J.A. Arter, J. Chappuis, and S. Chappuis. 2004. *Classroom Assessment for Student Learning: Doing It Right—Using It Well.* Portland, OR: Assessment Training Institute.

Tapscot, D. 2009. *Grown Up Digital: How the Net Generation Is Changing Your World.* New York: McGraw-Hill Books.

The Fluency Project. Available at http://21stcenturyfluency.com/about.cfm. Accessed February 22, 2010.

The MILE Guide: Milestones for Improving Learning and Education. Available at http://www.21stcenturyskills.org/documents/MILE_Guide_091101.pdf.

The Partnership for 21st Century Skills. 2010. Available at www.21stCenturySkills.org

The 21st Century Fluency Project. Available at http://21stcenturyfluency.com/fluencies.cfm. Accessed February 22, 2010.

White, Stephen. 2005. *Beyond the Numbers.* Englewood, CO: Lead + Learn Press.

SECTION 3
Leadership

Data Teams from a Principal's Perspective

A PRACTICAL LENS

"Leading knowledgeably means bringing all teachers to a high level of pedagogical effectiveness; but more than that, it means fostering interactions that keep teachers at that level through continuous application and refinement."

FULLAN, 2008*

Ms. Lauren Campsen uses strong leadership to guide her school to high levels of success. Ms. Campsen tells the story of the transformation of Ocean View Elementary School as a result of using the Data Teams process.

What does strong, active leadership look like in your school? How is the leadership in your school supporting your Professional Learning Communities?

*Fullan, M. 2008. *What's Worth Fighting For in the Principalship*, second edition. New York, NY: Teachers College Press, p. 25.

CHAPTER 7

Data Teams from a Principal's Perspective

LAUREN CAMPSEN

*Basically, there's collecting data
and then there's using data.
What we did not do was use the data to drive our
instructional program. The consensus was that
the students needed to change—certainly not us.
We still were not providing focused, data-based
instruction and interventions for our students.*

Knowledgeable and Committed Leadership

No new educational initiative can be successfully implemented in any school without strong leadership. Unless the school principal is extremely knowledgeable and committed to the new philosophy, program, organizational or management shift, or instructional strategy, any change is doomed to failure. This is one of the main reasons why the landscape across school districts is littered with the husks of failed initiatives and programs. *School leadership can make or break any initiative.* New leadership can transform low-performing schools into basins of high student achievement. Likewise, highly successful schools and districts can stagnate and decline when a strong and committed leader leaves and is replaced with a weaker and less knowledgeable or committed leader.

Bold and Risk-Taking Leadership

Effective, *deep* implementation of data-driven decision making under an organization of school Data Teams first requires bold and visionary leadership.

School districts seeking to shift school management to the Data Teams model must begin by carefully selecting principals who are open to change, able to step outside their comfort zone, and willing to take big risks. These principals must be both visionary and transformational. They must be willing to challenge the status quo, leaping from "what is" to "what can be."

Once districts have selected these principals, they must be willing to invest in them, providing extensive professional development and support. This training must be well planned and systematic. Randomly sending a few principals to one session and then others to another, jumping from one training program to another and then not providing support for principals as they face challenges, is a recipe for failure.

Once trained, these principals must be given the freedom and support to implement the Data Teams model. School districts must stand firmly behind principals when the predictable resistance to change begins, not only from teachers, but also from central-office staff and parents. School districts must face the cold reality of strong opposition to change and the difficulty of the paradigm shift required when teachers are held accountable for student achievement. When blaming a student for his or her failure is no longer an option, when the data spotlight is aimed directly at the instructional program, and when teachers and administrators are asked to look in the mirror for the cause of low test scores, major staff push back is too often a predictable result. District leadership must be prepared for this and be willing to take some initial heat to provide the support that the principal must have if he or she is to move the school into Data Teams and instructional accountability.

Actively Involved Leadership

Additionally, leadership must come from a building principal who is actively involved in both Data Teams organization and program and instruction implementation at all levels. The principal must become an expert in data-driven decision making and Data Teams organization. There must be a place in the Data Teams organization where the principal is actively involved in data analysis, in discussion of nonproficient students, and in the development of strategies and assignment of resources, both human and material. A school leader *must* have an intimate knowledge of exactly what is happening in his or her building at all times. A principal must know what challenges are occurring, who needs more support (student or teacher), what additional resources are needed and how current ones are being allocated, and when to be ready to intervene before any potential roadblock becomes an obstacle to implementation. Delegating this responsibility to others who lack the inherent power of the office of the principal is a recipe for half-hearted implementation at best and total failure of the Data Teams initiative at worst.

The Journey of Ocean View Elementary School

At this point, I would like to share the story of my school, Ocean View Elementary School in urban Norfolk, Virginia. Since Ocean View was recognized in 2008 as a National No Child Left Behind Blue Ribbon School, I have been asked repeatedly how a school with our demographics (64 percent of students qualify for free and reduced lunches, we have a high transient rate, and both white and African–American populations are split at about 45 percent each) can have such high student achievement with little or no achievement gaps. In other words, how in the world did we take our school from low performing and non-accredited in 2002 to Blue Ribbon in 2008? The answer is strong Data Teams implementing systematic, data-driven decision making and intervention, intervention, intervention. Let me share Ocean View's story.

Like many schools in Norfolk and across the state of Virginia, Ocean View struggled during the first years of state-mandated accountability testing. Our proficiency scores remained low and flat during the first three years of this accountability testing because we simply continued to do more of what we were already doing. Teachers worked very hard but kept doing more and more of the same thing and, consequently, got the same results. When test scores didn't improve, students were blamed. The Ocean View staff simply did not believe in our students. The fallacy that poor urban children could not achieve at high levels had been ingrained into the culture of the school. Teachers had low expectations for their students and the students met those expectations.

However, I had spent many years as a reading specialist. My experience taught me that all children *can* learn to read, but it's often quite challenging to teach them. Another cold, hard fact that my staff needed to face is that our students were not going to change. We would continue to receive the same students, from the same families, from the same neighborhoods. We could not change our students. We needed to realize that, at Ocean View, we could only change what we could control and that was what we—the adults in the building—were doing. But how could we make that happen? I needed help.

Luckily, my school district, Norfolk Public Schools, was quick to recognize the need for change and provided support and opportunities for principals to study new, research-based strategies for changing what we were doing. In the summer of 2001, I joined a number of principals and central-office staff in Denver at The

Center for Performance Assessment (now The Leadership and Learning Center) for training in data-driven decision making. I came back to Ocean View full of great ideas for collecting, organizing, and using data to guide and improve instruction. I knew what I needed to do, but I faced a lot of push back. Change is very hard and teacher resistance was great. Teachers felt that their expertise as educators was in doubt. They were teaching. It was the students' fault that they weren't learning— not the teachers' fault. Many teachers constantly challenged each and every change, especially the idea that perhaps the way they were teaching a skill was not the best way for all of their students. The concept that student achievement data reflected a need for examining instruction rather than student ability and motivation struck at the core of their view of themselves as teachers. They pushed back hard. I was simply not bold and strong enough in the face of such massive resistance. I came to the hill that so many leaders climb and I did not push to the top. I did not fully implement my plan.

We did start frequent common assessments. We did create data notebooks to collect and organize this student assessment data. We did talk about the data, but too often that conversation focused on all of the outside factors over which we had no control (parents not helping, students not trying) rather than on what *was* happening in the classroom. Basically, there's collecting data and then there's using data. What we did *not* do was use the data to drive our instructional program. The consensus was that the students needed to change—certainly not *us*. We still were not providing focused, data-based instruction and interventions for our students. Courageous conversations about the impact of teacher instruction on student achievement never made the agenda. Our scores that year remained flat.

In the end, I had to accept that the responsibility for student achievement in my school rested squarely with me, the school principal. The lack of improvement in student achievement was a failure of my leadership to fully implement the data-driven, decision-making model. Teachers can't blame students for not learning when teachers are unwilling to improve their own instruction. Principals can't blame teachers for not implementing changes when principals are unwilling to stand firm in the face of opposition. I knew what I needed to do, but I simply did not get the job done. Ocean View did not have the bold, risk-taking principal it needed.

This was a time of reflection for me. I needed support, and the district provided that support. In the summer of 2002, I asked to join another group of administrators who were returning to The Center for training in the development of Data Teams. That training, along with my recognition that I needed to be bold and willing to take risks, led to the reorganization of Ocean View. Ocean View moved from the old, site-based management model to a data-driven, decision-making management model organized under Data Teams. Teachers who were open and ready for the big changes our school needed were handpicked for new Data Teams leadership positions and provided with extensive training in Data Teams that same summer. Ocean View fully implemented this new organizational model during the 2002–2003 school year.

Faced with strong teacher resistance, the new leadership team and I had to make some hard choices. Leaders cannot always immediately change beliefs or attitudes. What they can do is change behavior. I developed a list of non-negotiables that teachers were directed to follow, I constantly monitored implementation, and I employed consequences for noncompliance. It was a very long, difficult year, but it worked! Our upward trend in student proficiency started then. State accountability test scores jumped and Ocean View received full state accreditation in 2003! Our school made adequate yearly progress (AYP) in 2004 and we never looked back. Teachers began to see the value in data-based decision making. Ocean View teachers, always hard working and dedicated (if not always eager for change), saw the results of their efforts. High student achievement became the key to teacher buy-in.

Now, all decisions, from teacher assignments to scheduling to budget to instruction, are truly driven by student data that are collected and analyzed by school Data Teams in a consistent and systematic way. Everyone, especially me, is held accountable for student achievement. Content vertical Data Teams use student

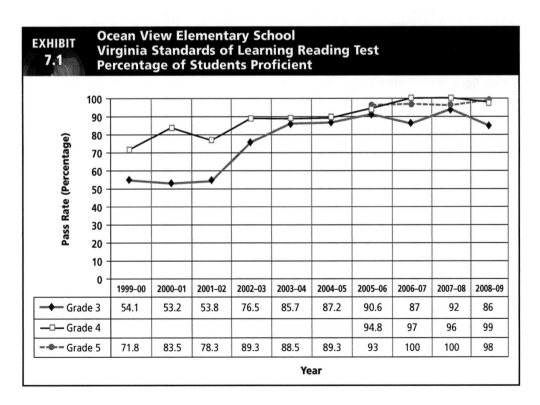

EXHIBIT 7.1

Ocean View Elementary School
Virginia Standards of Learning Reading Test
Percentage of Students Proficient

	1999–00	2000–01	2001–02	2002–03	2003–04	2004–05	2005–06	2006–07	2007–08	2008–09
Grade 3	54.1	53.2	53.8	76.5	85.7	87.2	90.6	87	92	86
Grade 4							94.8	97	96	99
Grade 5	71.8	83.5	78.3	89.3	88.5	89.3	93	100	100	98

Year

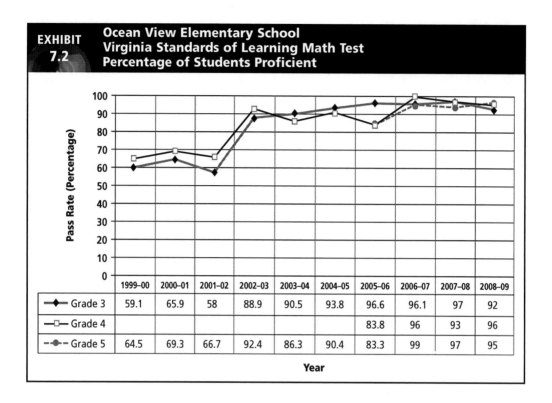

EXHIBIT 7.2

**Ocean View Elementary School
Virginia Standards of Learning Math Test
Percentage of Students Proficient**

	1999–00	2000–01	2001–02	2002–03	2003–04	2004–05	2005–06	2006–07	2007–08	2008–09
Grade 3	59.1	65.9	58	88.9	90.5	93.8	96.6	96.1	97	92
Grade 4							83.8	96	93	96
Grade 5	64.5	69.3	66.7	92.4	86.3	90.4	83.3	99	97	95

Year

data to develop instructional and intervention strategies that focus on specific individual student needs based on frequent common assessment data. They then track the effectiveness of their own strategies with more assessment data. The results have been dramatic.

Results

The journey was not easy, but, as Exhibits 7.1 and 7.2 confirm, the results in student achievement were dramatic. Note the jump in 2003, the year we fully implemented the Data Teams model.

This time I did what I knew needed to be done and, despite a lot of initial push back, today Ocean View students are achieving at high levels due to the instruction provided by teachers who *now* use student data to determine what interventions need to be done, and they hold *themselves* accountable for student achievement. At Ocean View, we have proven that demographics do not predict student achievement. Bold leadership made change happen. The resultant shift in staff beliefs and culture became the key to maintaining sustainability.

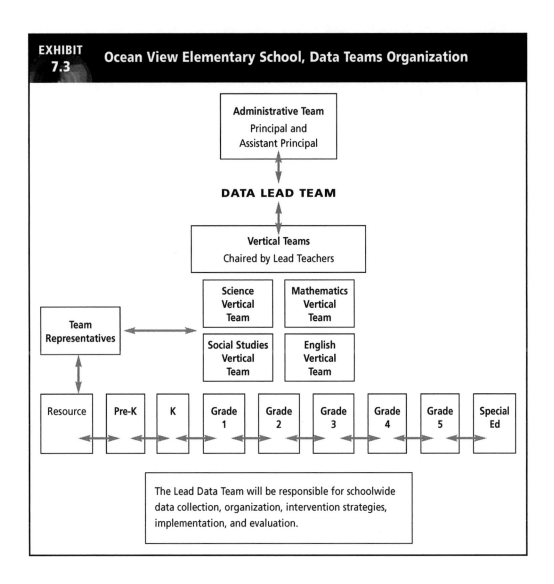

EXHIBIT 7.3 Ocean View Elementary School, Data Teams Organization

Administrative Team
Principal and
Assistant Principal

DATA LEAD TEAM

Vertical Teams
Chaired by Lead Teachers

Team Representatives

Science Vertical Team

Mathematics Vertical Team

Social Studies Vertical Team

English Vertical Team

Resource | Pre-K | K | Grade 1 | Grade 2 | Grade 3 | Grade 4 | Grade 5 | Special Ed

The Lead Data Team will be responsible for schoolwide data collection, organization, intervention strategies, implementation, and evaluation.

Centralized Versus Shared Leadership

Although the initial implementation of the Data Teams organizational model at Ocean View was a mandate from me, as was the selection of the original team leaders, this management model is now highly participatory. Every teacher in the school belongs to both a grade-level, horizontal Data Team and a content-area, vertical Data Team. Following the data-driven, decision-making model developed by The Leadership and Learning Center, these teams now analyze student assessment data, identify nonproficient students, develop instructional interventions, and monitor student progress on their interventions. Content vertical teams develop and implement schoolwide strategies. The leaders from these teams form the Ocean View Lead Data Team, which meets with me to oversee the entire instructional program at our school. Our whole leadership model, as well as our instructional program, was transformed.

Ocean View Elementary School Data Teams Organizational Model

At Ocean View, we are organized under a system of Data Teams in a data-driven, decision-making model:

- Grade-level, horizontal Data Teams meet weekly.
- Vertical Data Teams with members from each grade level, special-education classes, and resource staff members meet twice each month.
- The Lead Data Team with the principal, instructional specialist, vertical team leaders, and special-education member meets the first Friday of each month.

As Exhibit 7.3 shows, Ocean View is now governed completely by Data Teams.

As the school leader, I had to be brave enough to take bold risks. I had to be well informed and knowledgeable about all components of a Data Teams organization. I had to be committed to the new model. I had to be actively involved in its implementation. And, equally important, I had to remain involved and knowledgeable about every aspect of my school, my staff, and my students.

The Principal's Role in Meeting and Overcoming Obstacles and Challenges

The first, and often the most difficult, challenge to implementing Data Teams lies in teacher resistance to what really requires a paradigm shift in how we look at student achievement levels and place responsibility for the results. Data-driven decision making requires a belief that *all* children can learn regardless of the demographics of their background or the degree of their learning problems. When student achievement is low, blame can no longer be placed on the child. Instead, we must look to the instruction that the school and the classroom are providing to determine what must be done. We cannot change the children in our schools. What we can and must change is the education that we are providing.

Teachers do not always welcome a change that puts a spotlight on the academic levels of their students when they know that it will reflect on their instruction. Too often, they cannot let go of the belief that socioeconomics, ethnic origins, lack of parental support, or learning problems predict academic achievement. Sometimes, teachers have grown comfortable with teaching a certain way and resist changing even when their students are not demonstrating success. When a leader (school principal) directs a change, teachers often push back by arguing with the principal, talking against the initiative to colleagues, or simply going to their classroom, closing the door, and continuing to do what they have always done.

Faced with teacher resistance, the school principal must make some hard choices if Data Teams are to be fully implemented. Leaders cannot always immediately change beliefs or attitudes. What they can do is change behavior. The principal must be bold enough to develop a list of non-negotiables that teachers are directed to follow, provide extensive professional development, closely monitor implementation, and employ consequences for noncompliance.

The Principal's Role in Building Universal Accountability

At the core of data-driven decision making and Data Teams is the belief that all children can learn. The companion to that belief is the recognition that if all children can learn, then their inability to do so is not the failure of the students; rather, it is the failure of the school. Teachers and administrators can no longer play the blame game, always looking out the window for the cause of low student achievement. Instead, they must look in the mirror. This requires holding the adults in the building accountable for student achievement. It requires a culture of "no excuses" and a willingness to accept responsibility. *It requires a leader who first holds him or herself accountable for student achievement and who then holds his or her staff equally accountable.*

What does universal accountability look like? Data Teams provide the perfect framework for accountability. As Data Teams move through the data-driven decision making process, they must face the brutal facts of student achievement data and look for the root causes of poor achievement. Instruction that is not working must be identified and discarded or revised. Instructional strategies in high-performing classrooms must be discussed and implemented throughout the school. Principals must be willing to have courageous conversations with teachers of low-performing classrooms, to direct and monitor implementation of proven successful strategies, and to act when teachers fail to follow directions. The principal must clearly set the bar for high expectations, both for students and for teachers.

The Principal's Role in Professional Development

Successful, deep implementation of data-driven decision making in a Data Teams organizational model cannot happen without comprehensive professional development. Successful leaders recognize that fear of the unknown is often the greatest deterrent to change. Initial training before attempting implementation is an important key to success. School principals must find the time, the funding, and the expertise to provide that training. Once the model is implemented, refresher training must occur as new teachers join the staff and as experienced teachers begin to lose focus. At Ocean View, all new teachers are mentored in the data-driven, decision-making process, and all team leaders receive refresher training every other summer. The principal's role is to recognize that need and to ensure that professional development is ongoing, focused, and data driven.

The Principal's Role in Allocation of Human and Material Resources

Too often, limited school resources, both human and material, are squandered due to lack of central planning. Nonessential, prepackaged programs, unneeded equipment, and poorly used materials are bought for carelessly thought-out reasons. Likewise, human resources are often used in nonproductive ways. Highly skilled support-staff members are often used to substitute in classrooms, monitor hallways, create reports, and do clerical jobs instead of providing direct support to teachers and students.

The principal must be willing to make hard and sometimes unpopular decisions to ensure that all purchases and scheduling of staff time are driven by student achievement data. Once again, Data Teams provide the perfect framework for providing the essential information needed for making these choices. During team discussions of student assessment data, team members can focus on using data to identify student needs with regard to materials and interventions. The principal can then ensure that all purchases are directly linked to requests made by Data Teams that can use student assessment data to justify the need.

Also, once again, the principal's role in scheduling and assigning responsibilities to staff is critical and closely linked to Data Teams decisions. Rather than delegating master scheduling to a subordinate, the principal, as the instructional leader, must be actively involved, ensuring that instructional time is protected and that support-staff assignments are linked to student needs as determined by Data Teams. The principal must establish the importance of following schedules by monitoring and intervening in cases where schedules are not met.

The Principal's Role in Maintaining Program Fidelity

Finally, when a school reaches that hard-won goal of creating a school where Data Teams collect, discuss, analyze, and use student data to drive all instructional decisions, where all purchases and scheduling are determined by student-data-identified needs, and where no one can predict how students will perform based on their demographics, then the challenge of maintaining program sustainability and fidelity begins. Once again, leadership is vital. The principal must be constantly vigilant: monitoring for complacency, providing thoughtful and extensive training for new teachers and refresher professional development to veterans, refusing to delegate critical roles, and always keeping staff focus on student achievement and on the organizational model of Data Teams that leads to high student performance.

Bold, Transformational Leadership

The importance of strong, bold leadership in the implementation of a Data Teams management model in a school cannot be overemphasized. The use of student assessment data to shape and drive the entire instructional program in a school is most effectively done through Data Teams that operate in an environment of shared leadership with the school principal. This principal must be an expert in data-driven decision making. He or she must be actively involved in data analysis, scheduling, and allocation of resources. He or she must have a firm belief in the ability of the students to learn and must set high expectations for the achievement of each and every one of them. He or she must hold both him or herself and the entire staff accountable for that high student achievement. Finally, the principal must recognize what needs to be done, be willing to stand firm in the face of opposition, and have the vision and the courage to fully implement the Data Teams model. The principal must be a transformational leader.

Data Teams and
the Superintendent's Role

A PRACTICAL LENS

*"Leadership is about change—
how to justify it, implement it,
and maintain it."*

REEVES, 2006*

Mr. Stephen Ventura shows us how effective leadership can help us focus on the right initiatives. He convinces us that Data Teams are a replicable practice, one that will lead to increased student learning.

Mr. Ventura created "contagious, constructive energy" in his district by implementing Data Teams. **When have you been involved in a change that had unstoppable momentum?**

*Reeves, D.B. 2006. *The Learning Leader: How to Focus School Improvement for Better Results*. Alexandria, VA: ASCD, p. 158.

CHAPTER 8

Data Teams and
the Superintendent's Role

STEPHEN VENTURA

When faced with a challenge, look for a way, not a way out.

DAVID L. WEATHERFORD

One of the most important aspects of school improvement is the collection and organization of student performance data. More importantly, schools that analyze data make better decisions about which practices to replicate, improve, and change. But in order to truly reap the benefits of data collection and decision making, there must be a systematic, continuous process designed to maximize results.

Many school systems have an abundance of student performance data that is stored in data warehouses and only accessed by administrators or district leadership teams. Often, these data serve only one purpose: to inform others about student progress. The focus is on effect, or student outcomes, rather than on cause or on adult teaching behaviors.

In contrast, members of effective Data Teams know that, in order to increase achievement, there must be a commitment to analyze data regarding both cause *and* effect. The connection between instructional strategies and assessment results must be studied with total candor and with a no-fault reflection on professional practice.

Putting the Pieces Together

As a district level leader, it is important to understand which practices and services will have the greatest impact on student achievement. It is equally important to understand which data set will yield the best feedback to replicate successful practice and overcome obstacles, how to analyze those data, and how data can give us the authority to change and improve our instructional focus. When teaching

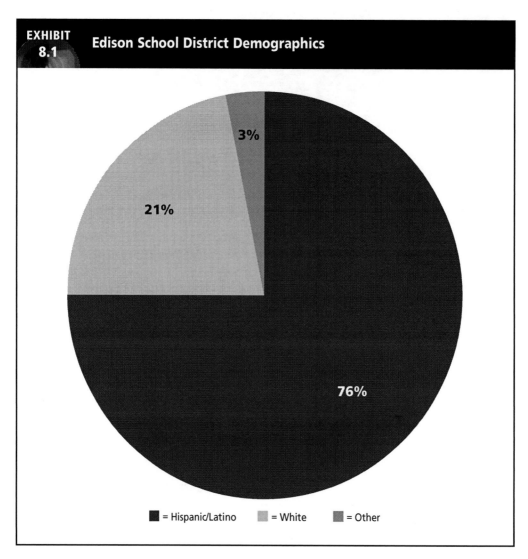

EXHIBIT 8.1   Edison School District Demographics

3%

21%

76%

■ = Hispanic/Latino   ▦ = White   ▦ = Other

professionals meet in small collaborative teams with a data set that is meaningful and manageable, it helps them address the needs of all students.

What we have discovered is that school improvement can be actualized through the Data Teams process because it provides a forum for the effective use of assessment results. The Data Teams protocol helps make sense of the data that we must process, and it differentiates between *talking* about data and actually *using* data. After reviewing student assessment results with pre– and post–Data Teams implementation, we realize that the Data Teams process has simply become the way we do business because the protocol helps stakeholders with every element of teaching and leadership.

In this chapter, you will see how we introduced four professional practices, *one at a time*, to maximize effectiveness and proper implementation. Fundamental to achieving breakthrough results in student achievement is a commitment to teamwork, openness to new strategies, and the participation of all staff in the effort. As a result of this model, the marked improvement in student achievement permitted teachers and leaders to discover that these initiatives work. Results-oriented practices define what we can influence and are accepted with enthusiasm and anticipation.

Our Story

Like many districts in California, we have seen a shift in student population and demographics (Exhibit 8.1). However, the gap between our student subgroups remains remarkably close. That is, all subgroups performed relatively *low* on state summative tests, including white students. There is no one group significantly outperforming another. For example, the percentage of students scoring "proficient" or higher in mathematics is 31.7 percent for Hispanic or Latino and 28.9 percent for white, not of Hispanic origin. Proficiency scores are determined by California Standards Test (CST) results.

The Academic Performance Index (API) report provides information about whether California schools and districts meet state requirements under the Public Schools Accountability Act (PSAA) of 1999. The API is a score awarded to schools and districts based on state summative test results. The API ranges from 200 to 1,000, with 800 designated as the statewide target. Exhibit 8.2 shows the API for the Edison School District.

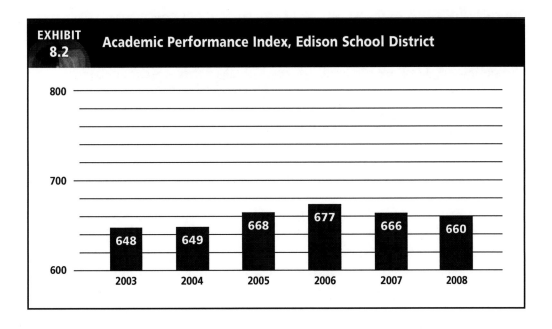

EXHIBIT 8.2   Academic Performance Index, Edison School District

	2003	2004	2005	2006	2007	2008
	648	649	668	677	666	660

The overall growth in the Edison School District experienced from 2003 to 2008 is only twelve points (648 to 660). According to the API growth model of at least 5 percent growth *per year*, it would take the district several years to reach a score of 800. Improving student achievement is our most urgent need. Although well intentioned, a 5 percent growth rate is simply not enough to dramatically increase student success. To be fair, the district did experience positive growth from 2004 through 2006. Successful replication of this growth could not be sustained, and it is unclear what strategies were implemented to achieve this increase.

For reference, the API growth formula simply subtracts the current API score (660) from the statewide target (800) and then multiplies by 5 percent. Therefore: $800 - 660 \times .05 = 7$ points of growth.

Like many other states, California places schools and districts on "watch lists" when they do not meet yearly growth targets over time. These schools and districts typically receive monitoring from well-intentioned and knowledgeable external support providers. Our district believes that our internal instructional initiatives have the greatest impact on student achievement. Our external provider agrees.

Leadership and Implementation

Leaders who are able to significantly increase achievement in their school systems share similar leadership behaviors. They are well aware that accomplishment begins with a focused set of initiatives that can provide short-term wins and long-term impact.

Providing opportunities to reduce the number of initiatives by determining the ones that matter the most, and providing regular and timely feedback, are all characteristics of effective leadership. Effective leaders also recognize that it makes no sense to introduce new initiatives until at least one or two ineffective, time-consuming programs are removed. The psychological advantages of implementation are increased when teachers and other stakeholders realize that, in order to accomplish something significant, other tasks deemed insignificant or ineffective must be discontinued. Once teachers and administrators recognize that they have the authority to take action, they can address the difference between tradition and necessity. In other words, it's time to stop implementing programs and practices that do not work.

When we studied our student performance data over time, we realized that we had to create a set of prioritized initiatives that addressed our current academic needs. Thus, *only four* were selected because we know something: Quality programs do not equate to mountains of written plans and complex expectations. Quality programs have the greatest impact on student achievement and teacher professional practice. Our four initiatives were:

- Decision Making for Results
- Priority Standards and "Unwrapping" the Standards
- Common Formative Assessments
- **Data Teams**

We were thoughtful about the order of implementation and how each initiative would complement and support districtwide strategies. Consequently, these four initiatives were implemented, one after the other, in the order in which they are listed. Each new initiative was dependent upon previous learning and provided participants with the prerequisite skills necessary to reinforce and increase their awareness of leadership, teaching, and learning. Our final initiative, Data Teams, was the culmination of all prior learning and provided a vehicle to combine the very best data analysis, feedback, and accountability. Each initiative was maximized through the implementation process.

Decision Making for Results

This process provided teachers and leaders with a systematic approach to increase their awareness of data that are worth collecting and analyzing. As each step unfolded, we continued to gain a deeper understanding of the application of data and learned how to apply that understanding to the process of improved decisions about our schools and district. We learned that student assessment data must address student needs rather than satisfy policy or compliance. Therefore, data must not only inform what students in the system are doing but help pave the way to monitor teaching and leadership practices as well.

A benefit of the Decision Making for Results process was the proliferation of grade-level or content-area goals and strategies in the form of an action plan. Action plans represent a commitment by the adults to change their instructional teaching behaviors and implement best practices. Action plans can be time consuming, but we didn't have to start the planning process from scratch. One of the best resources for strategy creation and implementation is Marzano's *Classroom Instruction That Works* (2001). Teachers use this resource to assist with strategies that are designed to support improvement goals. Once grade-level and content-area goals and strategies are created, action plans are distributed, copied, enlarged, and posted at all school sites as a focal point. They are referred to all year long and are posted in close proximity to data walls, which also act as points of reference, justification, and accountability.

Our action plans consist of four major components:

1. A focused specific, measurable, achievable, relevant, and timely (SMART) goal that targets a subject area, grade level, and student population

2. Three research-based instructional strategies that are action oriented and help learners overcome obstacles

3. Results indicators that are designed to monitor the degree of implementation and the effectiveness of the strategies

4. A list of persons responsible, resources that are utilized, and beginning and ending dates

When combined, we produce documents using the format shown in Exhibit 8.3.

EXHIBIT 8.3   Action Plan Steps and Schedule, Edison School District, 2009–2010

Content Area __ELA__   Grade __5__   School: Orangewood School   Edison Middle School

Targeted Goal 1 (what the students will do):
The percentage of all fifth-grade students, based on current Writing Strategies scores, will increase from 44 percent to 54 percent correct by the end of the 2009–2010 school year as measured by the California Standards Test administered in April 2010.

Strategies (What Adults Will Do)	Results Indicators (Measurement and Accountability Tool)	Persons Responsible, Resources, Start and End Dates
Teachers will provide nonfiction writing prompts of one or more paragraphs to summarize science or social studies concepts a minimum of once each week.	If teachers provide nonfiction writing prompts in social studies or science content areas, then we will see increased writing opportunities and higher writing scores.	Fifth-grade team *Classroom Instruction That Works*, social studies and science teacher's manuals September 2009–April 2010
Once per quarter, teachers will exchange a representative sample of student papers to grade based upon an applied rubric.	If teachers exchange a sample of student work and apply a scoring guide and/or rubric, then there will be consistent application of scoring and an agreement on what "proficient" work looks like.	Fifth-grade team *Classroom Instruction That Works*, social studies and science teacher's manuals October 2009–April 2010
The teachers will model peer-editing techniques for a specific writing convention once per quarter.	If teachers model peer-editing techniques, then students will accurately identify peer mistakes a minimum of 70 percent of the time.	Fifth-grade team *Classroom Instruction That Works*, Scott Purdy October 2009–April 2010

Because all plans feature actions driven by data, they are monitored on a regular basis through classroom visitations and assessment results and are then adjusted to produce desired outcomes.

Priority Standards

After building on successful implementation of data-driven decision making and action plans, it was time to decide what to teach within our instructional year. To do this, we simply replicated the pioneering work of author Larry Ainsworth (*Power Standards* [2003a] and *"Unwrapping" the Standards* [2003b]). It makes sense to go deeper with a fewer number of concepts and skills rather than to try and

---

| **EXHIBIT 8.4** | **Sample of Writing Priority Standards** |

Essential Standards Worksheet   Local Accountability Professional Development Series—Edison School District
Content Area: Math   Grade Level: 6

Team Members: Slikker, Richie, Menzies, Apperson   Number of Essential Standards: 11
Number of Essential Standards on district assessments:
Number of Essential Standards assessed on benchmark

CALIFORNIA CONTENT STANDARDS
Mathematics
Grade 6

NUMBER SENSE

Standard #	Original Language	Student-Friendly Language	Questions
1.3	Use proportions to solve problems (e.g., determine the value of N if 4/7 = N/21, find the length of a side of a polygon similar to a known polygon). Use cross-multiplication as a method for solving such problems, understanding it as the multiplication of both sides of an equation by a multiplicative inverse.	*I can use proportions to solve problems.* *I can understand and use cross-multiplication as a method for solving problems.*	(6)
2.3	Solve addition, subtraction, multiplication, and division problems, including those arising in concrete situations, that use positive and negative integers, and combinations of these operations.	*I can solve addition, subtraction, multiplication, and division problems using positive and negative integers.* *I can use combinations of operations to solve problems.*	(6)
1.4	Calculate given percentages of quantities and solve problems involving discounts at sales, interest earned, and tips.	*I can calculate percentages of quantities.* *I can solve problems involving:* *Discounts at sales* *Interest earned* *Tips*	(5)

superficially cover everything. An example of writing priority standards is provided in Exhibit 8.4. As you can see in this exhibit, the priority standards are written using the original standards language as well as student-friendly language.

The question of how to identify priority standards can be answered by applying three simple filters:

1. What do our students need for success in life?

2. What do our students need for success in school?

3. What do our students need for success on the state test?

When we asked teachers to consider these filters to select the standards that matter the most, they placed an "L" by those standards that are required for life, an "S" by those standards that are required for school success, and an "ST" by those standards that are required for our state summative test. When all three filters were selected for one standard, we knew that we were on to something. This sparked additional collaboration among teachers and helped build initial consensus about what the Power Standards should be for a particular grade level.

Perhaps the most rewarding aspect of prioritizing standards was when teachers looked for and established alignment between grade levels before and after their own. This classic exercise to discover gaps and omissions from one grade level to the next provided some of the best teamwork I have observed during my time as an

EXHIBIT 8.5   Happy Teachers Who Prioritize and Align Power Standards

administrator. The opportunity to collaborate with different grade levels to pursue a common purpose, the ability to make cross-grade determinations, and the sense of accomplishment and pride provided the enthusiasm to ensure our implementation of prioritized learning targets. As depicted in Exhibit 8.5, teachers are quite happy when they can prioritize and align Power Standards.

"Unwrapping" the Standards

To effectively manage our Power Standards, we selected a process to identify the concepts and skills within each standard. The main benefit of "unwrapping" a standard is to develop the deepest understanding of what to teach and assess. This is an essential step when designing instructional units that will eventually be analyzed based on common formative assessment results.

"Unwrapping" standards is much more than simply underlining nouns (concepts) and circling verbs (skills). Done properly, this process helps to determine higher cognition by pinpointing what students must know and be able to do. Teachers select standards that are the most critical for student success. The purpose for "unwrapping" those standards is to provide teachers with a "first step" opportunity to examine state standards and determine essential concepts and skills. When "unwrapped" standards are presented in a graphic organizer, they become concrete and provide educators with an opportunity to identify what is necessary to make a difference in student achievement.

You will see how Power Standards and "Unwrapping" the Standards are absolutely indispensable as they provide a standards-based foundation for common formative assessments.

Common Formative Assessments, Scoring, and Feedback

"Schools with the greatest improvements in students achievement consistently used common assessments."

DOUGLAS REEVES, ACCOUNTABILITY IN ACTION, 2004

The implementation of Common Formative Assessments relies heavily on the expectations of leaders and how committed they are to seeing this process to fruition. Leaders must provide time and support in order to see the benefits of this initiative. Formative assessments are key to providing the rich data set necessary for an effective Data Team meeting. Used correctly, they can help discern the difference between assessments that do not diagnose student-learning needs and instructional effectiveness and those that do.

Many teachers now realize the difference between a benchmark assessment and a formative assessment. Benchmark assessments are given at the end of an instructional unit, while formative assessments are given *through* an instructional unit. The latter produces information that allows for instructional adjustments. Additionally, teachers have more opportunities to select effective teaching strategies based on a regular and frequent assessment system. Benchmark assessments are summative in nature and provide a final status report, leaving little or no opportunity to make midcourse teaching corrections. Please do not be confused about benchmark assessments. They are an integral part of an assessment system yet prove to be the most effective when they are intentionally designed to support formative assessments.

More than anything, there must be complete alignment of Power Standards and Common Formative Assessments. The purposeful selection of essential standards and the unwrapping process provides a sharp focus for instructional units and assessment.

Our year one implementation focused on designing assessments for a single content area (mathematics). This strategy was important on a number of different levels:

1. Process-oriented implementation provided time to become familiar with the development of common formative assessments and to build support.

2. Focus on a single content area helped to create a degree of consistency of instruction.

3. Assessment results were timely.

4. Teachers spent more time on instruction that was designed to drive student achievement results as opposed to creating multiple content-area assessments in an academic year.

We administer two assessments per month. These pre- and post-assessments are collaboratively designed by grade level and content area and are based on the concepts and skills from each "unwrapped" standard. They let us know if there are students who, at the beginning of a year or unit, already know and understand certain key concepts and skills. This information is essential for differentiated instruction, because it provides solutions for both low- and high-achieving students.

Our assessments are largely comprised of multiple-choice items, which are the most popular type of selected-response assessments. However, it is beneficial to use more than one type of assessment, such as constructed response and essay. The benefit of the selected-response format permits us to score assessments quickly while providing varying degrees of difficulty. As we refine our assessment system, we will transition to more balanced assessments that combine selected and constructed response along with short essays.

Scoring

I am often asked how teachers find time to score multiple assessments per month, use item-analysis tools to evaluate and determine the validity of specific test items, and provide timely and effective feedback to students.

Even in a relatively small district, assessments can accumulate. For instance, our district processes more than 24,000 formative assessments per year! This number will double when we begin to administer assessments for language arts. With the acquisition of scanning software and a data technician to process pre- and post-test answer documents, our teachers are not responsible for correcting assessments—only for *analyzing them*. They receive detailed reports that sort student achievement, standard by standard, allowing the opportunity for stronger data focus and improvement goals. This commitment from the central office demonstrates breakthrough structures for sustainability and systemwide improvement.

Prior to automated scoring, teachers worked collaboratively to develop scoring guides and determine proficiency levels based upon the academic needs of students. These teacher-generated rubrics were then paired with our scanning software to create the performance criteria necessary for consistent scoring. This rubric was shared with students in a specific language so that they, teachers, and parents all understood what "proficiency" meant.

Feedback

Without question, student feedback about assessment results is critical, even if that feedback is not attached to a letter grade. Our students receive feedback in a timely enough manner so that students can associate the feedback with the work that generated the feedback. In some instances, students who receive feedback without an attachment to a letter grade actually perform at a higher level. This is because they know that their assessment results are categorized without bias.

Data walls (Exhibits 8.6 and 8.7) contain internal data, including classroom assessments, but they also contain external data, such as state test scores. This powerful and transparent display of progress fosters continuous collaboration throughout the year. Data walls also provide effective feedback that consists of five key characteristics:

1. It is **accurate:** If feedback is not accurate, then it cannot be used.

EXHIBIT 8.6 Example of a Data Wall Displaying Pre- and Post-Assessment Information, Allowing Students to Be Included in the Assessment Process

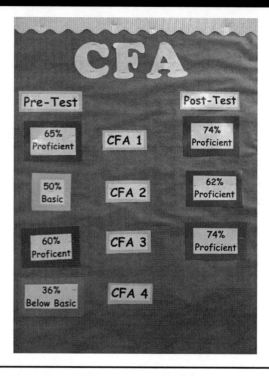

EXHIBIT 8.7 Larger Data Walls, Designed to Communicate Common Formative Assessment Results Schoolwide, With Results Posted for All to See (Including Parents)

2. It is **timely**: If feedback is provided too late, we miss an opportunity to improve achievement.

3. It is **fair**: The same performance deserves the same feedback.

4. It is **understandable**: Is the feedback provided using student-accessible language?

5. It is **effective**: Can feedback be used right away in order for students to increase their performance?

Now that we have established a system for common assessments, scoring, and feedback, it is time to create a method for collecting and analyzing assessment results.

Data Teams

The combination of Decision Making for Results, Power Standards, "Unwrapping" the Standards, and Common Formative Assessments provides a solid foundation for the introduction and implementation of Data Teams.

The use of Data Teams is a powerful practice that permits teachers to set improvement goals based on student achievement data. Data Teams meetings reduce teacher isolation, increase collaboration, and provide a level of consistency to help team members address issues and questions related to reading, writing, and mathematics.

Our Data Teams meetings occur on a monthly basis. They are conducted under one roof and include the entire academic team. This promotes accountability and encourages a purpose-driven collaboration. Grade levels meet together, and those who teach extracurricular activities are included in the process dependent upon their expertise. Our Data Teams are not limited to academic data analysis. They also encompass other areas of student needs, including attendance and behavior.

The bottom line is that constructive energy is contagious. It is not uncommon for grade levels to venture into "other academic worlds" with the intention to learn and replicate instructional strategies. This becomes cross-curricular collaboration, because it is common professionalism to exchange successful practices and agree upon what needs to be enhanced in the name of student achievement. The Data Teams protocol simply combines the best practices of all prior initiatives!

Data Teams implementation requires us to modify school schedules in order to provide time for teachers to meet. Meetings are scheduled once per month on early student-release days. During this two-hour time period, teachers analyze data and set improvement goals during the first hour and write common formative assessments during the second hour. Depending on the Data Teams cycle, assessments are written to prepare for the next unit of instruction. Our pre- and post-assessments are intentionally aligned. Doing so prevents distortion in grading, because the same skills and concepts must be assessed prior to teaching and after teaching.

Each grade level and content area has a Data Teams facilitator. These leaders are responsible for gathering assessment results and preparing those results for the rest of the team. They strictly adhere to the Data Teams five-step process:

1. Collect and chart data

2. Analyze strengths and obstacles

3. Establish SMART goals

4. Select instructional strategies

5. Determine results indicators

This structure fosters the core purpose of a Data Teams meeting: to focus on the effectiveness of teaching and learning.

Data Teams facilitators meet periodically with school principals. These meetings help administrators receive important feedback about assessment and instruction. They are informed about assessment methods, effective instruction, and student proficiency percentages. Principals realize that Data Teams facilitators are not administrators. Therefore, principals support facilitators in the event that any team personnel issues arise. The facilitator is a leader and a peer. Dealing with uncooperative team members and other interference that impedes the process is handled exclusively by the site administrator.

Parallel Processing and Task Switching

Parallel processing is the ability to carry out multiple operations or tasks simultaneously. I use this term in the context of human cognition, particularly in the ability of the brain to simultaneously process incoming stimuli. For example, parallel processing allows us to read a book and listen to music at the same time. Airline pilots are especially adept at parallel processing because of their ability to control the aircraft while simultaneously monitoring instruments, communicating with the control tower, and maintaining situational awareness.

Task switching is defined as rapidly moving back and forth between different activities while only being able to execute those activities one at a time.

I equate these definitions and examples to leadership decisions and how they can either send mixed and confusing messages or clear, meaningful pathways. When leaders look at deep implementation of specific initiatives, it would be wise to consider the benefits of parallel processing. Within reason, parallel processing can actually increase efficiency, especially if one activity is a routine and complements the other.

For instance, the relationship between Common Formative Assessments and Data Teams (*see* Exhibit 8.8) suggests a relatively parallel formation of two initiatives that, when implemented simultaneously, can increase efficiency *and* achievement. Both are sound, research-based strategies, and together they provide a powerful alliance in determining instructional practices that lead to better results.

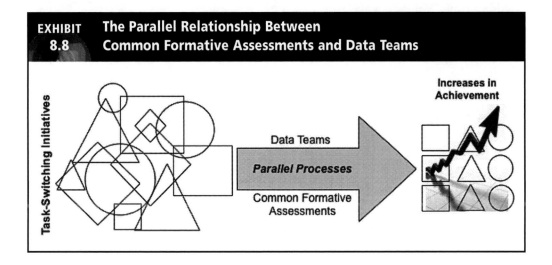

EXHIBIT 8.8 The Parallel Relationship Between Common Formative Assessments and Data Teams

Task switching, on the other hand, can decrease mental efficiency, especially if the tasks are cognitively demanding. Shifting attention, as is often the case in education, undermines initiative development, and those switches cost time and efficiency, especially if an initiative is new or unfamiliar.

In terms of academic achievement, random selection of programs that are not aligned can keep schools and districts from acquiring their achievement goals because of constant switching between different instructional initiatives. Leaders must recognize the benefits of initiative implementation by choosing programs that build success because of their parallel relationship. Teachers will be less stressed, students will see connections between learning, and focused implementation will yield increased results.

Is It Working?

When schools improve instruction, curriculum, assessment, feedback, and leadership, they improve student achievement. It really is that simple. The acid test for success is not how many programs you implement; it's the degree of implementation that is the most important variable when comparing achievement results to initiatives. We know that, to have any impact at all on student achievement, we must have all stakeholders involved in deep implementation. This means that physical education teachers, counselors, music teachers, and other specialized educators must be a part of the entire process. Fifty percent of the faculty does not comprise "all stakeholders" or critical mass. To realize the benefits of any initiative, there must be 80 to 100 percent implementation; otherwise, we might as well not implement anything at all. *The only meaningful difference between an initiative, like Data Teams, and increased levels of student achievement is the degree of implementation.*

Results

This section highlights pre- and post-initiative implementation and compares student achievement scores accordingly.

The No Child Left Behind Act identifies a district as a Program Improvement Local Education Agency (LEA) if it does not meet adequate yearly progress (AYP) goals for two consecutive years. To determine this status, improvement is focused primarily on academic achievement in English-language arts and mathematics. Our district has not been able to exceed AYP requirements.

Exhibit 8.9 represents achievement results over time. It illustrates proficiency scores and correlates increased scores with implementation. It is important to realize the *cause* of this improvement. We believe that the correlation between the implementation of Power Standards, Common Formative Assessments, and Data

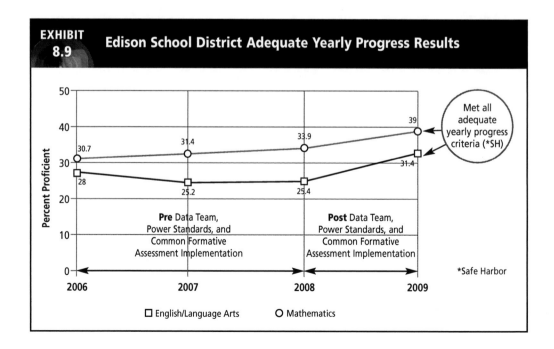

EXHIBIT 8.9   Edison School District Adequate Yearly Progress Results

Teams helps to predict achievement. In other words, these antecedents are highly connected to improved performance.

Because students in our school who performed below the "proficient" level in either English-language arts and mathematics decreased by at least 10 percent from the percentage of the preceding school year (2008), our current AYP results are strong enough to lift us out of "program improvement." In order to accomplish

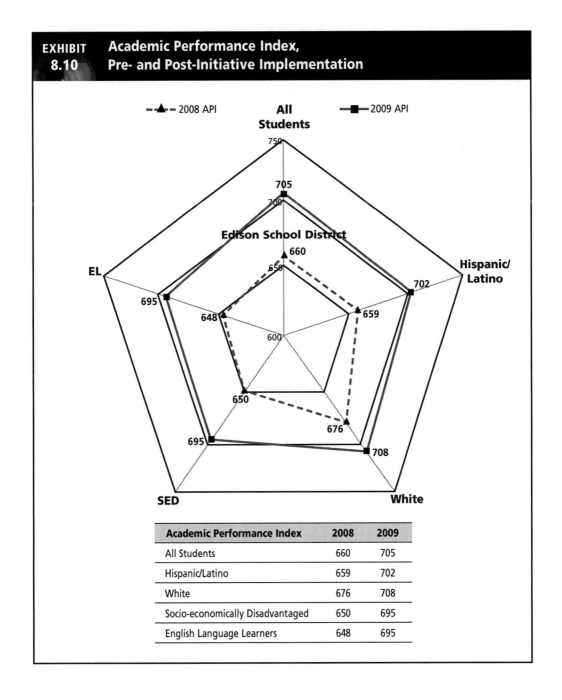

EXHIBIT 8.10	Academic Performance Index, Pre- and Post-Initiative Implementation

Academic Performance Index	2008	2009
All Students	660	705
Hispanic/Latino	659	702
White	676	708
Socio-economically Disadvantaged	650	695
English Language Learners	648	695

this, we must sustain this improvement for two consecutive years. Scores from 2009 indicate that all AYP targets for all subgroups have been satisfied. Admittedly, this is an alternative method of meeting annual measurable objectives (AMOs), but it is a method that meets federal accountability requirements.

Whether or not we meet static growth targets, we know what we must keep doing.

Exhibit 8.10 displays multivariate observations between student subgroups and the Academic Performance Index (API). The higher the API, the closer each set of scores is pushed toward the rim of the chart. Each spoke of the chart represents a variable, in this instance, a student subgroup. The inside portion of the chart plots 2008 API scores for each group of students. Scores between subgroups are somewhat consistent in terms of achievement, with the exception of the white student subgroup. This group of students scored an API higher than other subgroups (676). All 2008 subgroup scores represent achievement prior to initiative implementation.

API scores for 2009 are plotted outside of 2008 scores and represent an average increase of forty-two points across all subgroups. Additionally, we discovered that the differential between the highest scoring subgroup (white students) and lowest scoring subgroup (English Learners) decreased from twenty-eight points (2008) to thirteen points (2009) (Exhibit 8.11). Both groups experienced significant gains in post-implementation achievement.

The 2009 API scores demonstrate a consistent pattern of gap-closing achievement. *All* student subgroups exceeded their 5 percent growth target, and gaps in achievement between subgroups were significantly reduced.

Our 2009 district API score increased by *forty-five* points, leaving little doubt that focused implementation of critical initiatives can have an enormous impact on achievement (Exhibit 8.12). Exceeding a score of 700 marks a new era of achievement and success. Sharing these results with teachers and students creates a sense of

EXHIBIT 8.11	Differential Between White Students and English Learners, 2008–2009		
Academic Performance Index	2008 White Students	2008 ELL	Difference
2008 Scores	676	648	–28 points
Academic Performance Index	2009 White Students	2009 ELL	Difference
2009 Scores	708	695	–13 points

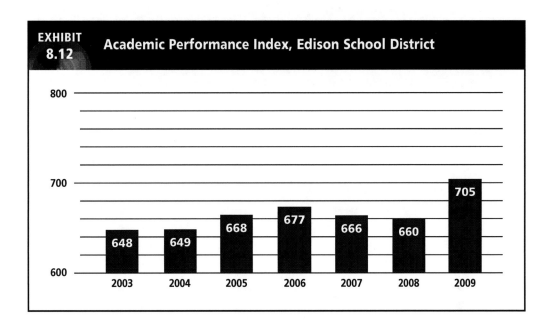

EXHIBIT 8.12   Academic Performance Index, Edison School District

Year	API
2003	648
2004	649
2005	668
2006	677
2007	666
2008	660
2009	705

pride, accomplishment, and satisfaction. By the way, to meet the API requirement for AYP purposes, a school or an LEA must demonstrate a growth of at least *one* point, or a minimum API score of at least *650*.

You, Too, Can Replicate This Process

The purpose for writing this chapter is to convince you that this process can be replicated. Schools and districts invest millions of dollars each year to purchase programs designed to increase achievement. This chapter is not about programs; it's about professional practice. As educators, we must recognize the difference between the two. For every dollar we invest in the competence of teachers and leaders, we will net a greater gain in student achievement than if we were to spend that money on another program. Initiatives discussed in this chapter can be implemented for a fraction of the cost of programs and fads. Programs typically lose sustainability when there is a change in faculty and leadership. Sound professional practice never goes out of style.

Implementation is free. When educational organizations determine the most important practices and are committed to sustaining those practices, costs will actually decrease because of better-informed resource allocation and drastic reduction in student failures. It will no longer be necessary to have students repeat courses, retake exit exams, or create extra programs for students who drop out.

The ideas presented here provide you with a structure to create and sustain your own school improvement. These practices can be applied in any school of any size, regardless of demographics and economics. With determination and focus, and a belief that this is work worth doing, it can become the culture of your school or district and will ultimately lead to improved student learning.

References

Ainsworth, L. 2003a. *Power Standards*. Englewood, CO: Lead + Learn Press.

———. 2003b. *"Unwrapping" the Standards*. Englewood, CO: Lead + Learn Press.

Gasser, U., and J. Palfrey. March 2009. "Mastering Multitasking." *Educational Leadership*, vol. 66, no. 6, pp. 14–19.

Marzano, R., D.J. Pickering, and J.E. Pollock. 2001. *Classroom Instruction That Works*. Alexandria, VA: ASCD.

No Child Left Behind. Available at http://ed.gov/nclb/landing.jhtml. Accessed April 20, 2010.

Reeves, D.B. 2004. *Accountability in Action,* second edition. Englewood, CO: Lead + Learn Press.

Weatherford, D. 2009. *The Writings of David L. Weatherford*. Available at http://www.davidlweatherford.com. Accessed March 20, 2010.

Accountability and the Data Teams Process

A PRACTICAL LENS

> *"The purpose of educational accountability is the improvement of teaching and learning. It is a constructive process in which successful results can be associated with specific teaching and leadership practices so that teachers and leaders can be recognized and their successful practices can be replicated."*
>
> **DOUGLAS REEVES, 2004***

Dr. Connie Kamm shows us how Data Teams flourish in a Comprehensive Accountability Framework as they embrace reciprocal accountability and distributed leadership.

Dr. Kamm helps us to see the link between Data Teams and accountability frameworks. **How does your accountability system sustain high levels of teaching and learning by embracing collaboration through Data Teams or Professional Learning Communities?**

*Reeves, D.B. 2004. *Accountability in Learning: How Teachers and School Leaders Can Take Charge.* Alexandria, VA: ASCD, p. 8.

CHAPTER 9

Accountability and the Data Teams Process

CONNIE KAMM, Ed.D.

*Through an emphasis on a collective vision, clear alignment,
and individual contributions through deep collaboration,
a Comprehensive Accountability Framework provides a
structure and context for transformative change.*

The Context for Shared Accountability

Over the past four decades, education worldwide has undergone an intense examination of its very nature and quality. As Sir Ken Robinson (2009) points out in *The Element*, "Nearly every system of public education on earth is in the process of being reformed—in Asia, the Americas, Europe, Africa, and the Middle East" (p. 235). With this reform has come an increasing demand for evidence of student learning and, as a result, the development of standardized tests focused on prescribed outcomes for student achievement—mainly in literacy, mathematics, and science. These mandated tests have become the primary focus of education in many countries. This era of high-stakes testing and often rigid curricula has been accompanied by accountability protocols that name and shame errant schools that are not meeting the mark. Unfortunately, as Hargreaves and Shirley (2009) note in *The Fourth Way*, the data used to evaluate schools' success are often "defined and operationalized narrowly, simplistically, and unthinkingly" (p. 33).

Accompanying this emphasis on measuring and reporting standards mastery is the gnawing awareness that the world has entered a new era, a global community, powered by a Web-enabled playing field where current standards of learning emphasized by national and local governmental agencies may not ensure students' future successes.

Futurist Glen Hiemstra, author of *Turning the Future Into Revenue* (2006), tells a story of a train track in a rural area that is intersected by a road. At this intersection there are no crossing arms, no bells, and no flashing lights to warn drivers of the approach of a speeding train. Instead, a sign is posted at this intersection of tracks and road that reads: "This train takes exactly 21 seconds to pass this point whether you're on the tracks or not." Hiemstra draws an analogy between this speeding train and the future. Like the train, the rapid changes demanded by the twenty-first century have arrived abruptly, unannounced to many, and are demanding an immediate response. We can choose not to act and, consequently, be run over by this train of the future. We can become passengers on this train. Or, better yet, we can become engineers on the train of the future. In bringing this anecdote to education, schools are challenged daily with the responsibility to prepare today's students to be engineers on this train of the future by challenging and supporting students' learning in relevant and engaging ways that prepare them for future success. Ultimately, it is this task for which educators are accountable.

The demands of educating youth with the skills to be successful in the global community of this digital age, paired with a continued climate of current educational accountability, causes many educators to feel overwhelmed. As a result, leaders in education are struggling to find ways to arm themselves and their colleagues with the knowledge and structures necessary to rethink leadership and teaching practices; to engage students in expansive learning experiences; and to design meaningful, collaborative assessment practices.

In this complex and pressured environment of educational reform, one thing is clear—accountability for student learning must be shared by all stakeholders (students, teachers, administrators, school board members, parents, and the larger community). Furthermore, this commitment to systemwide accountability, which leads to deep and relevant learning, is most effectively sustained by a Comprehensive Accountability Framework that supports

- A continuous cycle of collaborative planning

- Deep implementation of research-based strategies

- Frequent monitoring at all levels: districtwide, schoolwide, and in teacher-based teams (Data Teams)

An Overview of a Comprehensive Accountability Framework

In a research review titled "How Leadership Influences Student Learning," Leithwood et al. (2004) state that to optimize a flourishing culture of learning:

Successful educational leaders develop their districts and schools as
effective organizations that support and sustain the performance of
administrators and teachers, as well as students. Specific practices
typically associated with this set of basics include strengthening
district and school cultures, modifying organizational structures,
and building collaborative processes (p. 9).

At the heart of a Comprehensive Accountability Framework are protocols and
processes that lead to deep collaboration and unite all stakeholders in a district
toward the accomplishment of one vision—optimal student learning. A
Comprehensive Accountability Framework builds a structure for shared leadership
and aligns the collection and analysis of data from a systemwide focus to classroom
application. The rigorous development of a Comprehensive Accountability
Framework involves a design team—a districtwide group of stakeholders
comprised of school board members, community leaders, parents, administrators,
and teachers (including union leaders). This diverse team composition:

- Ensures multiple points of view

- Creates legitimacy for the work

- Secures a level of readiness and a sense of shared responsibility

- Stimulates momentum for change

As the design team experiences the development and implementation of a
Comprehensive Accountability Framework, its members establish a systemwide
commitment to sound leadership practices, improved instruction, and exemplary
student learning.

The components of a Comprehensive Accountability Framework are displayed
in Exhibit 9.1. Reading from left to right, this framework is anchored in the **Vision,
Mission,** and **Strategic Goals** of a district. In many districts, these statements are
just words posted on the wall and populating Web sites. When a district imple-
ments a Comprehensive Accountability Framework, these words are put into action
through a rigorous curriculum that is aligned with prioritized standards and
through clearly designed strategies that focus on optimizing student learning at all
levels. School systems that embrace this accountability approach collect and analyze
data on a variety of levels in order to ensure that they are moving toward their
vision and accomplishing their goals. The following measurements or indicators,
from state tests to individual classroom assessments (formal and informal), are
displayed on the right side of Exhibit 9.1:

- **Classroom Assessments:** Classroom formative assessments (informal and
  formal) are generated by teachers and serve as frequent indicators of

individual student mastery of priority standards. The results of these indicators are used to inform instruction and to guide students as they set personal goals for deeper learning.

- **Data Team Common Formative Assessments**: Common formative assessments are generated and analyzed by grade-level and content-area Data Teams, to measure student mastery of priority standards within specific units of instruction. The results of these assessments are viewed collaboratively by the Data Teams and are used to guide the implementation of effective instructional strategies that ensure learning for all students.

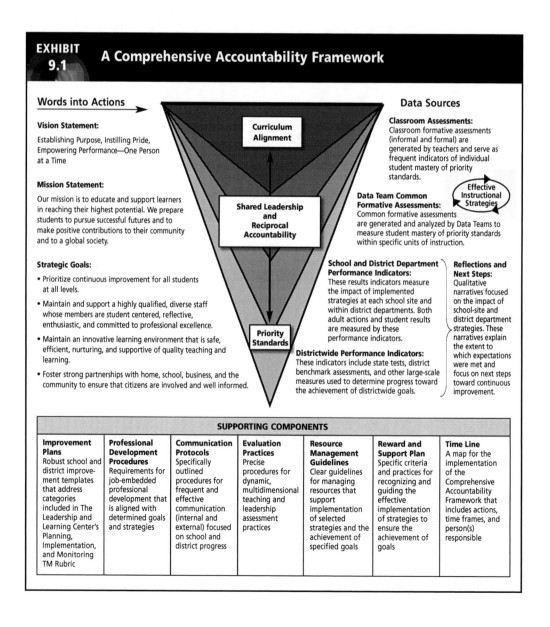

EXHIBIT 9.1   A Comprehensive Accountability Framework

Words into Actions

Vision Statement:

Establishing Purpose, Instilling Pride, Empowering Performance—One Person at a Time

Mission Statement:

Our mission is to educate and support learners in reaching their highest potential. We prepare students to pursue successful futures and to make positive contributions to their community and to a global society.

Strategic Goals:

- Prioritize continuous improvement for all students at all levels.
- Maintain and support a highly qualified, diverse staff whose members are student centered, reflective, enthusiastic, and committed to professional excellence.
- Maintain an innovative learning environment that is safe, efficient, nurturing, and supportive of quality teaching and learning.
- Foster strong partnerships with home, school, business, and the community to ensure that citizens are involved and well informed.

Curriculum Alignment

Shared Leadership and Reciprocal Accountability

Priority Standards

Data Sources

Classroom Assessments: Classroom formative assessments (informal and formal) are generated by teachers and serve as frequent indicators of individual student mastery of priority standards.

Effective Instructional Strategies

Data Team Common Formative Assessments: Common formative assessments are generated and analyzed by Data Teams to measure student mastery of priority standards within specific units of instruction.

School and District Department Performance Indicators: These results indicators measure the impact of implemented strategies at each school site and within district departments. Both adult actions and student results are measured by these performance indicators.

Districtwide Performance Indicators: These indicators include state tests, district benchmark assessments, and other large-scale measures used to determine progress toward the achievement of districtwide goals.

Reflections and Next Steps: Qualitative narratives focused on the impact of school-site and district department strategies. These narratives explain the extent to which expectations were met and focus on next steps toward continuous improvement.

SUPPORTING COMPONENTS						
Improvement Plans Robust school and district improvement templates that address categories included in The Leadership and Learning Center's Planning, Implementation, and Monitoring TM Rubric	**Professional Development Procedures** Requirements for job-embedded professional development that is aligned with determined goals and strategies	**Communication Protocols** Specifically outlined procedures for frequent and effective communication (internal and external) focused on school and district progress	**Evaluation Practices** Precise procedures for dynamic, multidimensional teaching and leadership assessment practices	**Resource Management Guidelines** Clear guidelines for managing resources that support implementation of selected strategies and the achievement of specified goals	**Reward and Support Plan** Specific criteria and practices for recognizing and guiding the effective implementation of strategies to ensure the achievement of goals	**Time Line** A map for the implementation of the Comprehensive Accountability Framework that includes actions, time frames, and person(s) responsible

- **School and District Department Performance Indicators**: These performance indicators measure the impact of implemented strategies at each school site and within district departments. Both adult actions and student results are measured. At schools, the indicators may include the percentage of teachers who are implementing a determined strategy with fidelity as well as the results of schoolwide or Data Team assessments. In district departments, the indicators may include data collected about the timeliness of completed work orders. These indicators are viewed frequently in order to determine necessary midcourse corrections.

- **Districtwide Performance Indicators**: Districtwide indicators include state tests, district benchmark assessments, and other large-scale measures used to determine progress toward the achievement of districtwide goals. All district stakeholders are aligned in their work toward improved performance on these indicators.

The series of four triangles in the center of Exhibit 9.1 are inverted to symbolize a reverse in the hierarchical model heretofore practiced in education. The data that reveal the most granular detail about individual student learning come from the classroom. When classroom teachers are given the opportunity to collaboratively share the results of common teacher-generated assessments in a Data Team context, they are provided with a supportive structure in which they can learn improved practices from one another to bring into their classrooms.

The next supporting layer involves the efforts of all school and district staff members to set goals and implement strategies that will enhance and deepen learning in the classroom. The base triangle represents large-scale state and district assessments. Although these assessments can provide a big picture of student achievement, they are not intended to provide teachers with day-to-day information about individual student growth in learning. This series of inverted triangles represents not only the increasing specificity of evidence of student learning but also enforces the belief that there must be a districtwide awareness of and support for the core student learning that is taking place in classrooms.

It is critical that educators align and focus this influx of data so that all stakeholders can use the information from key data sources to make sound instructional decisions that positively impact individual student learning. At the same time that educators study this evidence of student learning, they continue to grow professionally as well. One major component of this continuous learning cycle is noted in the "Reflections and Next Steps" section at the far right of Exhibit 9.1. The reflective narratives explain the extent to which expectations were met and focus on next steps toward continuous improvement. The practice of building reflection into the data analysis procedures within a Comprehensive Accountability Framework ensures that data are not noted just for the sake of looking at data; rather, data are analyzed in order to change and improve practice.

In order to further ensure the successful implementation and sustainability of a Comprehensive Accountability Framework, thorough Data Team guidelines and protocols are also included within the framework. The structures of Data Teams, the sequence of meetings, the process that is followed to generate and analyze assessment results, and the determination of effective instructional strategies are clearly addressed within the framework.

To support the critical actions of measuring and responding to student learning needs, the following components (noted at the bottom of Exhibit 9.1) are also included within the Comprehensive Accountability Framework:

- **Improvement Plans**: These plans consist of robust school and district improvement templates that address each of the categories included in The Leadership and Learning Center's research-based Planning, Implementation, and Monitoring TM (PIM) process (see Appendix 1). They include SMART goals and strategies for reaching these goals, which are grounded in a comprehensive needs analysis that is supported by research and that focuses on student learning.

- **Professional Development Procedures**: These procedures contain clearly stated requirements for research-based professional development practices that include theoretical understandings, modeling, embedded practice and feedback, and on-the-job coaching and reteaching. The professional development opportunities are in alignment with stated goals and strategies.

- **Communication Protocols**: These protocols are specifically outlined procedures for effective and frequent (at least quarterly) communication with both internal and external stakeholders. This communication focuses on school and district progress toward the achievement of goals. Progress is based on the results of indicators that measure both adult implementation of research-based strategies as well as student achievement.

- **Evaluation Practices**: These practices include dynamic, multidimensional teaching and leadership assessments that contain rich performance rubrics. The rubrics address multiple domains of effective practice and support self-reflection and continued growth.

- **Resource Management**: These guidelines provide clear structures for managing resources that support the achievement of strategic goals. They address the allocation and management of the district's resources—people, time, money, and programs—and ensure the successful implementation and sustainability of selected strategies that focus on improved student learning.

- **Reward and Support Plan:** The reward and support section encompasses specific criteria and practices for recognizing and guiding the effective implementation of strategies to ensure the achievement of goals. The purpose of the reward plan is to acknowledge the implementation of strategies that have led to successful student learning; the intent of the support plan is to provide necessary assistance when goals included in improvement plans are not achieved.

- **Timeline:** This guide provides a map for the implementation of the Comprehensive Accountability Framework that includes actions, time frames, and person(s) responsible.

In *Getting Serious About School Reform: Three Critical Commitments*, Robert Marzano (2008) notes that the historical structure of schools "might be characterized as 'loosely coupled'—individual schools within a district and individual teachers within a school operate in total autonomy and isolation" (p. 2). Marzano goes on to state that "until districts and schools become 'tightly coupled' regarding student achievement, they cannot be thought of as serious about school reform" (p. 2). A Comprehensive Accountability Framework ensures this tight coupling between districts, schools, Data Teams (teacher-based teams), and individual educators to ensure learning success for all.

In *Leading Change in Your Schools: How to Conquer Myths, Build Commitment, and Get Results*, Douglas Reeves (2009) writes that "the paradox of change leadership is the elevation of a vision far greater than the individual and, at the same time, the elevation of the individual to a place that is unique, powerful, and essential" (p. 6). Through an emphasis on a collective vision, clear alignment, and individual contributions through deep collaboration, a Comprehensive Accountability Framework provides a structure and context for transformative change.

Reciprocal Accountability and Distributed Leadership

The success of a Comprehensive Accountability Framework is reliant on the principle of reciprocity. In *Bridging the Gap Between Standards and Achievement: The Imperative for Professional Development in Education*, Richard Elmore (2002) explains this principle of reciprocal accountability:

> For every increment of performance I demand from you, I have an
> equal responsibility to provide you with the capacity to meet that
> expectation. Likewise, for every investment you make in my skill
> and knowledge, I have a reciprocal responsibility to demonstrate
> some new increment in performance. This is the principle of
> "reciprocity of accountability for capacity." It is the glue that, in the
> final analysis, will hold accountability systems together (p. 5).

Reciprocal accountability is a systemwide commitment. By subscribing to a Comprehensive Accountability Framework, all stakeholders (administrators, teachers, staff members, students, parents, and members of the larger community) are responsible to one another to ensure increased student learning and improved practice. In "A Balanced School Accountability Model: An Alternative to High-Stakes Testing," Ken Jones (2004) writes: "For a balanced model of school accountability to succeed, there must be a system in which states and districts are jointly responsible with schools and communities for student learning. Reciprocal accountability is needed: one level of the system is responsible to the others. . . ." (p. 598).

In adopting the principle of reciprocal accountability through a Comprehensive Accountability Framework, school districts make the commitment to recognize the worth of each person in the system as an active and vital member of a team. In *School Reform from the Inside Out: Policy, Practice, and Performance*, Richard Elmore (2006) states that the purpose of leadership is to improve instructional practice and performance, regardless of role. The collaborative processes ensured by the implementation of a Comprehensive Accountability Framework expand the definition of educational leadership beyond the sole domain of district and building administrators. Leadership is shared by school and district improvement teams, Data Teams, and individual staff members. Leaders who are highly successful develop and count on leadership contributions from many others in their organizations. This more inclusive paradigm of leadership embraces a distributed leadership model.

The practice of distributed leadership overlaps with those of *shared, collaborative, democratic,* and *participative* leadership. All of these terms signal a model of leadership that assumes a set of practices that "are enacted by people at all levels rather than a set of personal characteristics and attributes located in people at the top" (Fletcher and Kaufer, 2003, p. 22). This movement toward distributed leadership shifts attention to "what school personnel do, more than who is doing it, and challenges the conventional belief that leadership is associated with particular positions" (Scribner et al., 2007, p. 4). At the heart of distributed leadership is the "recognition that tapping into the ideas, creativity, skills, and initiative of all or the majority of those in a group or organization unleashes a greater capacity for organizational change, responsiveness, and improvement" (Woods, 2004, p. 5).

Under a distributed leadership model, educators are provided with the opportunity to work closely with one another, making inferences about the results of student work and exploring effective practices to support student learning. Educators respond with a high degree of satisfaction to this collaborative work that results from a distributed leadership model.

This satisfaction is evident in a recent interview with five members of a fifth-grade Data Team from Berea Elementary School in the Valley Central School District in New York and their principal, Hope Stuart. Throughout the interview, the teachers and the principal registered their extreme satisfaction with their opportunity to share in the leadership of their school and to learn from one another. Stuart noted that, in participating collaboratively in the school improvement process, they all engage in the deliberate practice of using data to pinpoint specific student learning needs. She goes on to observe that teachers are now teaching with a purpose and are using evidence of student learning daily to adjust instruction and provide rich feedback to students. In *Visible Learning: A Synthesis of Over 800 Meta-Analyses Relating to Achievement*, John Hattie (2009) notes that "the biggest effects on student learning occur when teachers become learners of their own teaching and when students become their own teachers" (p. 22). This practice is definitely evident at Berea.

During the interview, the teachers noted that they "all have ownership and are seeing the results." Berea is showing steady growth in both language arts and math, with a cohort increase in grades three through five from 2 percent to 17 percent in English language arts scores over the past three years. Eighty-eight percent to 92 percent of all third- through fifth-grade students passed the New York State Math Assessment in 2009. With this schoolwide conversation grounded in evidence of student learning, Tara, one of the fifth-grade team members, stated, "My teaching is more focused. I don't teach the same thing year after year. I teach what the children need." Amy, a fifth-grade teacher, noted the change to the shared leadership model, stating, "I have never worked so hard or been more rigorous in my instruction. Seeing the results of what students are achieving is phenomenal, and that makes me so proud to work with the professionals that I am with. I am very happy."

In *The Fourth Way: The Inspiring Future for Educational Change*, Hargreaves and Shirley (2009) state that research on happiness points out that "the three things that make people happy are purposes, empowerment, and relationships" (p. 73). The authors elaborate on these three components of happiness connecting their comments to educators:

Teachers feel positive emotions when their *purposes* are clear, focused, and achievable, and when those purposes belong to them.... Second, teachers, like other people, feel happy when they experience being *empowered*, in control of their work lives, and not at the beck and call of others. Last, happiness comes from developing and achieving purposes in positive *relationships* with colleagues and others, whereas, unhappiness springs from a professional life that provides no time to develop or sustain any relationships at all. Inspiring purposes developed and achieved with others are the foundation of successful and sustainable educational change (p. 73).

"Purpose, power, and relationships" sum up the experiences of educators who work in a district that unifies all stakeholders in support of a single vision of rich learning for all students through the implementation of a Comprehensive Accountability Framework.

The Data Teams Connection

Reciprocal accountability and distributed leadership, inherent in a Comprehensive Accountability Framework, are perhaps the most clearly evident in the work of Data Teams—grade-level or content-area teams of teachers. In most schools, the practice of teachers working in isolation has been the norm. One of the drawbacks of this practice is that teachers have not had the structure and support necessary to challenge their thinking about effective teaching practices or to learn new approaches to teaching and learning from one another. Data Teams break this cycle of isolation by involving educators within schools in critical conversations focused on student learning results and effective instructional practices. One of the major benefits of Data Teams is in the rich teacher collaboration that occurs. Through this collaborative process, Data Teams build strong, professional communities in schools. They promote shared accountability for student learning and establish norms of collegiality among teachers that are associated with higher levels of student achievement (Lee and Smith, 1996; Louis, Marks, and Kruse, 1996; Newmann and Wehlage, 1995).

In a recent conversation, four members of a biology team from Aptos High School in the Pajaro Valley Unified School District in California registered their extreme satisfaction with their opportunity to share in the leadership of their school and to learn from one another through Data Teams collaboration.

The Pajaro Valley Unified School District is in the final stages of completing a

Comprehensive Accountability Framework. Within the context of their framework, they have built collaborative structures for continuous improvement throughout the district, including Data Team work. In reference to collaboration, Gretchen, a new biology teacher at Aptos High School, pointed out that the opportunity to collaborate with her peers has been "incredible." She stated that she feels very fortunate to sit down with veteran teachers who are teaching the same thing so that they all learn from one another. Bob, a biology teacher and the science department chair, pointed out that trust, friendship, and respect are evident in the science department. This culture of collegiality nurtures rich collaboration. As a veteran teacher, Bob also explained how much he is learning from his colleagues about powerful strategies for teaching. He states that exploring lesson development and discussing transparent analysis of results with colleagues provides a fantastic culture for developing professionals. Mark, another veteran member of the science department, added that he feels "incredibly lucky" to have a collaborative culture in the science department all of the time. He concurred that gaining knowledge about teaching from his colleagues is a very positive experience. Jake, another veteran member of the group, agreed, stating that their collaborative work has "a lot of value."

Data Teams, like the biology group at Aptos High School, meet frequently—at least twice monthly—to generate standards-based common formative assessments, analyze their students' results, and share differentiated and engaging research-based strategies to implement in their classrooms. These communities of professionals engage in powerful conversations responding to the following questions:

- Which priority skills and concepts do students need to master to be successful in their future?

- Which research-based strategies will we use to ensure that each student has mastered these priority skills and concepts?

- How can we effectively engage students to be active participants or leaders in their own learning?

- How will we assess that each student has learned the targeted skills and concepts?

- What interventions will we establish to provide lifelines for students who are not proficient in essential skills and concepts?

- How will we enrich the learning of students who are already proficient before instruction begins?

By participating in Data Teams, educators are empowered to collaborate as scholars engaged in research. Teachers not only generate questions about teaching and learning—they also state hypotheses about instructional practice and the impact of that practice on student achievement. Teachers implement the determined practice in their classrooms and collect the evidence in terms of student assessment results. Data Teams provide the opportunity for shared reflection based on student performance, which then leads to the informal and formal publication of effective practices.

Establishing Data Teams builds "the kind of relational trust in schools that helps teachers set aside the structures that protect their autonomy and relax the cultural barriers to collaborative action" (Halverson, 2006, p. 4). This teacher-based team process builds a culture of inquiry where teachers are challenged to engage in reflection and analysis that lead to more effective practice and, as a result, to greater student achievement. Data Teams are a crucial link in districts that are committed to reciprocal accountability for student achievement under the guidelines of a Comprehensive Accountability Framework.

In order for Data Teams to be successful, districts and schools must establish a culture where these teams or professional communities can flourish. In "Policies that Support Professional Development in an Era of Reform," Darling-Hammond and McLaughlin (1995) point out that:

> Habits and cultures inside schools must foster critical inquiry into teaching practices and student outcomes. They must be conducive to the formation of communities of practice that enable teachers to meet together to solve problems, consider new ideas, [and] evaluate alternatives ... (p. 6).

Resources such as time and quality professional development are essential in ensuring the efficacy of Data Teams. It is through a powerful Comprehensive Accountability Framework that the support for implementing and sustaining Data Teams is ensured.

Comprehensive Accountability Framework: A Winning Strategy for Student Improvement

In *Implementing Change: Patterns, Principles, and Potholes*, authors Gene Hall and Shirley Hord (2005) note that leaders of effective change decrease the isolation of the staff, build its collective capacity, nurture positive relationships, and impel "the unceasing quest for increased effectiveness so that students benefit" (p. 193). A Comprehensive Accountability Framework establishes a powerful organizational structure that distributes change leadership among district stakeholders. It aligns and unifies district teams, school teams, and Data Teams toward the accomplishment of systemwide goals. Through a commitment to collaboration, the frequent analysis of data, and a dedication to continuous improvement, the implementation of a Comprehensive Accountability Framework ensures dynamic learning opportunities for all students.

References

Darling–Hammond, L., and M.W. McLaughlin. 1995. "Policies That Support Professional Development in an Era of Reform." *Phi Delta Kappan*, vol. 76, no. 8, pp. 597-604. Available at http://web.ebscohost.com.ezproxy1.lib.asu.edu/ehost/detail?vid=3&hid=101&sid=c1f95798-79f8-4fe2-bdba-e251e3f31d4a%40sessionmgr106. Accessed September 26, 2007.

Elmore, R.F. 2002. *Bridging the Gap Between Standards and Achievement: The Imperative for Professional Development in Education.* Washington, D.C.: Albert Shanker Institute.

———. 2006. *School Reform from the Inside Out: Policy, Practice, and Performance.* Cambridge, MA: Harvard Education Publishing Group.

Fletcher, J.K., and K. Kaufer. 2003. "Shared Leadership: Paradox and Possibility." In C.L. Pearce and J.A. Conger (Eds.), *Shared Leadership: Reframing the Hows and Whys of Leadership,* pp. 21–47. Thousand Oaks, CA: Sage.

Hall, G.E., and S.M. Hord. 2006. *Implementing Change: Patterns, Principles, and Potholes,* second edition. Boston, MA: Pearson.

Halverson, R. 2007. "How Leaders Use Artifacts to Structure Professional Community in Schools." In L. Stoll and K.S. Louis (Eds.), *Professional Learning Communities: Divergence Depth, and Dilemma,* pp. 93-105. New York: Open University Press.

Hargreaves, A., and D.L. Shirley, eds. 2009. *The Fourth Way: The Inspiring Future for Education Reform.* Thousand Oaks, CA: Corwin.

Hattie, J. 2008. *Visible Learning: A Synthesis of Over 800 Meta-Analyses Relating to Achievement.* New York: Routledge.

Hiemstra, G. 2006. *Turning the Future into Revenue.* Hoboken, NJ: John Wiley & Sons, Inc.

Jones, K. 2004. "A Balanced School Accountability Model: An Alternative to High-Stakes Testing." *Phi Delta Kappan,* vol. 85, no. 8, p. 584.

Lee, V.E., and J.B. Smith. 1996. "Collective Responsibility for Learning and its Effects on Gains in Achievement for Early Secondary School Students." *American Journal of Education,* vol. 104, no. 2, pp. 103–147.

Leithwood, K., et al. 2004. *How Leadership Influences Student Learning. Review of Research.* New York: The Wallace Foundation. Available at http://www.wallacefoundation.org/KnowledgeCenter/KnowledgeTopics/CurrentAreasofFocus/EducationLeadership/Pages/HowLeadershipInfluencesStudentLearning.aspx.

Louis, K.S., H. Marks, and S.D. Kruse. 1996. "Teachers' Professional Community in Restructuring Schools." *American Educational Research Journal,* vol. 33, no. 4, pp. 757–98.

Marzano, R.J. 2008. *Getting Serious About School Reform: Three Critical Commitments.* Centennial, CO: Marzano and Associates.

Newmann, F.M., and G.G. Wehlage. 1995. *Successful School Restructuring: A Report to the Public and Educators.* Madison: University of Wisconsin–Madison, Center on Organization and Restructuring of Schools.

Reeves, D.B. 2009. *Leading Change in Your Schools: How to Conquer Myths, Build Commitment, and Get Results.* Alexandria, VA: ASCD.

Robinson, K. 2009. *The Element: How Finding Your Passion Changes Everything.* New York: Viking.

Scribner, J.P., et al. 2007. "Teacher Teams and Distributed Leadership: A Study of Group Discourse and Collaboration." *Educational Administration Quarterly,* vol. 43, no. 1, pp. 67–100.

Woods, P.A. 2004. "Democratic Leadership: Drawing Distinctions with Distributed Leadership." *International Journal of Leadership in Education,* vol. 7, no. 1, pp. 3–26.

APPENDIX 1

Planning, Implementation, and Monitoring (PIM™) Rubric

The following descriptions only provide a general overview of the components in the much more specific PIM™ rubric created by The Leadership and Learning Center. The actual PIM™ rubric is used for a thorough analysis of school and district improvement plans. In a Comprehensive Accountability Framework, these components inform the development of school and district improvement templates.

Planning:

Comprehensive Needs Analysis: A systematic and comprehensive analysis of the school's/district's instructional and organizational effectiveness (strengths and weaknesses) provides the foundation for the school improvement plan. Both cause and effect data are included in the analysis. Cause data focus on adult implementation of research-based strategies. Effect data focus on student learning results that reflect the impact of the adult actions.

Inquiry Process: Cause-and-effect relationships are determined, and the correlation between needs and strategies is identified. The focus is on a few vital issues that will have the biggest impact on student achievement. Root causes are routinely identified and addressed.

Specific Objectives (Goals): SMART goals guide school improvement (Specific, Measurable, Achievable, Relevant, and Timely).

Implementation:

Targeted Research-Based Strategies: All strategies are grounded in sound research and evidence that will demonstrate how strategies will support improved achievement. All strategies directly impact student learning.

Master Plan Design: A limited number of action steps are indicated and clear. Time lines are purposeful, and the capacity for midcourse corrections is indicated in the plan. Action steps designate the person(s) responsible, and necessary resources are clearly delineated.

Professional Development: Critical professional development strategies are aligned with school and district objectives. Teachers and administrators focus on effective instructional strategies that impact student achievement. A system is in place for coaching and mentoring that sustains the selected strategies.

Parental Engagement: Empowering ways to include parents in improving student achievement are identified and are employed frequently. Areas where parents might need training and education are also specified, and the provision of that training is differentiated to meet the needs of parents and their children.

Monitoring:

Monitoring: Explicit steps for monitoring progress toward the attainment of *all* school objectives are described. Multiple forms of data to be collected are clearly explained. Key people are designated who will monitor activities. A process for midcourse corrections and for reporting progress to the staff is indicated in the plan.

Monitoring Frequency: Frequent monitoring of student achievement is indicated by specific time lines. The monitoring schedule (> monthly) reviews both student performance and adult teaching and leadership practices.

Evaluation: Planned results are compared with achieved outcomes, and a specific improvement cycle is determined. A plan for next steps is included that specifies how strategies and outcomes will be communicated to all stakeholders.

SECTION 4

Supporting the Data Teams Process

Data Teams
as Professional Development

A PRACTICAL LENS

"We know what effective professional development looks like. It is intensive and sustained, it is directly relevant to the needs of teachers and students, and it provides opportunities for application, practice, reflection, and reinforcement."

DOUGLAS REEVES, 2010*

Dr. Kris Nielsen and Ms. Barb Pitchford illustrate the value of job-embedded professional development that focuses on the use of data and collaboration. They make a convincing argument that it is through collaboration, not isolation, that teaching and learning improve.

How does professional development in your school enhance teaching and learning? List the professional learning opportunities in your school. How are they driven by data, research, and collaboration?

*Reeves, D.B. 2010. *Transforming Professional Development into Student Results.* Alexandria, VA: ASCD, p. 23.

CHAPTER 10

Data Teams as Professional Development

KRIS NIELSEN, Ph.D.
BARB PITCHFORD

Improving practice can only be done by teachers,
not to teachers.

JUDY WURTZEL, 2007, P. 30

Isolation: The Enemy of Improvement

We teach so that students can learn. Test scores or not, our goal is to improve learning for all students in every subject, in every grade level, every day. Improved learning cannot occur without improved teaching. The improvement of teaching cannot occur without reflection, problem solving, and imagination. Certainly, these actions can occur without collaboration, but as we all know, "we" is smarter than "me."

Quality teaching is immeasurably enhanced by teacher collaboration. The adage of "just leave me alone and let me teach" is as old as the twentieth century, gone the way of landlines and Edsels. The model of professional practice in the twenty-first century is grounded in the concept of collaboration. As Arthur Wise (2004, p. 43) explains:

> Professionals do not work alone; they work in teams. Professionals begin their preparation in the university but do not arrive in the workplace ready to practice. They continue their preparation on the job. In medical, legal, and architectural settings, services are provided by experienced and novice professionals working together to accomplish the goal—to heal the patient, win the lawsuit, plan the building. The team delivers the services ... the novices learn by doing, with feedback and correction.

Thanks to the Internet, collaboration does not require proximity. We have seen powerful and productive teacher collaboration occur when the teaching team is separated by thousands of miles! In the remote regions of Alaska, teachers who teach the same subject in the same district are isolated by hundreds and sometimes thousands of miles, but cyberspace allows them to collaborate—generating plans, writing assessments, sharing data, developing interventions, and monitoring progress as frequently as they choose.

With baby boomers retiring and the annual teacher turnover rate reaching as high as 35 percent in some districts, it is even more essential that teachers work in teams to plan, assess, problem solve, and continually develop their knowledge and skills. For the neophyte, as well as for the veteran, learning from colleagues is the most powerful form of professional development. It is timely, relevant, shared, and provocative. It is a practice that requires rigorous professional dialogue, causes immediate instructional adjustment, and ensures ongoing support.

"How did you learn to teach?" We often ask that question of teachers and administrators across the country at all levels. More often than not, we may hear, "Well, they showed me my room and where the books were stored, and I was on my own." We suggest that the teaching profession take lessons from other professions; that is, provide ongoing, varied opportunities for inexperienced teachers to work with those who are suited to be mentors and supporters. Working in a Data Teams structure requires teachers to share practices and strategies that work, to identify those that do not, to dig deeper into the root causes of the results they are seeing, to explore the contextual framework of the practices, and to share in action research to find the best fit for their next steps. It is the heart of incremental and continuous improvement. Is this inquiry process a practice that teachers would regularly engage in alone? Our experience suggests that it does not happen regularly and frequently without strategic, scheduled collaboration.

Teachers' days are frantically busy from the minute they walk into the school building (and often earlier) to when they walk out. Teaching is both energizing and exhausting. Lack of time is the constant—time to see individual students, time to plan, time to return phone calls, time to evaluate assignments, and certainly time to collaborate. In order for intentional and efficient collaboration to occur in this time-starved environment, meetings must be scheduled and structured in an agreed-upon process. Without committed time and structure, we have seen Data Teams falter and stall out, not for lack of interest but for lack of movement. In a Data Teams structure, the data are connected to student faces and context—they tell a story. The heavy lifting involved in improving student achievement is facilitated easily when capacity is created and the burdens are shared. The insights provided by the work leads us to the very best answer for each learner.

One results indicator of a collaborative culture that we have observed is unsolicited testimonials of teachers. "We crave time to collaborate! Once a week is not enough!" we heard recently. We have seen teachers spontaneously gather together after administering a common formative assessment and immediately begin to brainstorm strategies to address the identified issues. The discussion focused on needs, challenges, and strategies, as well as on strengths in student work. The students in those classes immediately and directly reaped the benefit of teachers working as a Data Team. The chances of such immediate action and intervention occurring without the collaborative thinking facilitated by the Data Teams structure are slim. Synergy tackles the problem.

Caution: Isolation encourages mediocrity. Isolation allows for individual teachers to make choices about management, instruction, pacing, and interventions. Accountability is sporadic in such a system. With so much to do, so many students, and such limited time, decisions are made quickly and are not necessarily based on research, good practice, or experience. Collaboration immediately ramps up quality—it's just human nature.

Developing Collective Capacity

"... the most powerful professional development occurs
in real time around real problems in real schools
involving real people who actually have to make decisions
about what to do on a day-to-day basis."

RICHARD ELMORE, 2005, PP. 20-27

The power of an effective Data Teams structure lies in the capacity building that occurs in the midst of true collaboration. As we observed recently, an effectively collaborating team can, in a very short amount of time (in this particular instance, four teachers and thirty minutes), examine data, discuss strategies that have been successful and unsuccessful, and brainstorm assessment ideas to help them dig deeper into the underlying causes of the results. The team referenced here then divided tasks among themselves, set deadlines, and prepared to give a next short, formative pre-assessment that was designed to help provide answers to their specific questions about their students and direction for the next instructional steps.

Capacity consists of new competencies, new resources (time, ideas, expertise) and new motivation (Fullan, 2008). The vehicle for building capacity is a collaborative Data Team. Teachers who work together are likely to increase their individual and collective capacity to ensure that all children are learning at high levels.

"You cannot have students as continuous learners and effective collaborators without teachers having the same characteristics."

MICHAEL FULLAN, 1993

Pre-assessment is not a new idea for teachers. However, collectively designed pre-assessments that are administered in similar ways help to minimize external variables that impact results. Assessment variables such as unclear directions, lack of clarity in expectations, and environmental stressors can certainly skew results and may cause teams to make incorrect assumptions about student learning. As with instructional strategies, teams must address how they will administer formative assessments. After all, if resulting student data are what will determine the next steps in instruction, it is important to minimize the impacts that adults may inadvertently have on those results.

We recently worked with some schools that are embarking on an entirely new system of assessment. As students took a practice exam, it became clear that the true levels of their learning were not being measured because of testing variables that were entirely foreign to them. As we brainstormed these variables with principals, we realized that these factors would need to be addressed directly in order to ensure reliable results on assessments. Some of these included literacy skills (for exams that were not focused on measuring these), timed testing, unfamiliar vocabulary, text types (notably fiction versus nonfiction), skill at reading and processing directions (particularly if past assessment forms had included the reading of instructions to students), unfamiliar organization of text, diagrams or problems, and unfamiliar problem-solving strategies (displayed in selected-response items). A critical role of Data Teams is to question and discuss variables of all sorts that may impact assessment results.

Teams that formalize the discussion a bit further also strengthen the discussion. The question becomes, "What can we do for each student?" and dialogue becomes focused on problem solving and idea sharing, not on finding fault or on looking for external causes on which to focus.

Once data from a pre-assessment have been collected, the questions should really begin to flow. While it seems natural to immediately jump to the question of what to do with students who are achieving at different levels, the team facilitator must push the questioning beyond the obvious. For example:

- What common trends do we see in student work? Are there patterns of error or success that are surprising?

- What has been the previous experience of the student who falls into different levels of proficiency (including previous instructors, contexts, familiarity with key concepts that may have come from different classes or content areas, and strategies that the teacher may or may not have used consciously and deliberately)?

- Is the assessment itself a reliable measure? For example: Are questions misleading? Is vocabulary unfamiliar if vocabulary is not what is being assessed? Do different learning needs and styles interfere with performance?

As Dennis Sparks (2004) contends:

> ... any school faculty, working as a learning community, has all the intellectual resources it needs, right now, to vastly improve instruction and levels of learning. Outside expertise can be helpful; it is not essential. What's needed is for teachers to be given the mandate—and the time—to focus on common assessments, look at interim student learning results, and fine-tune their teaching accordingly. In this simple scheme, teachers themselves—not outside experts providing staff development—can become the primary source of improvement as they teach each other the practice of teaching ... the most important research is the research they themselves conduct with their colleagues.

Data Teams Develop Strategic Teaching

Truly effective Data Teams are focused on the complex task of developing, expanding, and growing strategic teaching. When the term "data-driven decision making" first made its way into the vernacular of education, there was a flurry of activity as school and district staff collected and compiled data, searched for tools to manage data, and began to make high-stakes test data public. The realization that something needed to change in accordance with the data collection was a bit slower in coming. The hard work is not the examination of the data or the compiling, charting, or communicating about the data. The push past the data to the adult actions that should follow the data is where the hard work lies.

The development of strategic teaching is complex. With the pull of textbooks, pacing guides, standards, and benchmarks, teachers often feel as if they have to move fast through content in order to keep up. In the current structures of schools, we observe that time is too often the constant and learning is the variable. Data Teams strive to work within the school structures (which are difficult to change for many reasons) to make learning the constant.

Collaborative structures such as Data Teams are critical for new teachers. In addition to working together to teach strategically and gleaning new ideas and learning during focused discussions, effective teams also build in the capacity for real-time, job-embedded, professional development. In a truly collaborative culture, it is accepted and, indeed, almost required, that team members ask for assistance with unfamiliar instructional strategies, methods, structures, and processes. They share materials and resource ideas as well as various areas of expertise. To take the learning a step further, teams that are given time to observe each other teaching to learn from each other and to provide collegial feedback truly maximize the learning of the whole team.

> *"It is virtually impossible for teachers to learn how to improve their practice if they can't watch each other teach."*
>
> RICHARD ELMORE, 2008, PP. 42–47

Search for Solutions

> *"The way a team plays as a whole determines its success. You may have the greatest bunch of individual stars in the world, but if they don't play together, the club won't be worth a dime."*
>
> ATTRIBUTED TO BABE RUTH

What is the point of creating and sustaining Data Teams? Why go to all the trouble and effort of organizing the teams and carving out the time for teams to meet? The power of the team is in finding the solutions to the challenges of teaching—searching for the answer to how to teach all students well. It is about changing the actions of the adults to change the results, to improve the learning, and to ensure student progress.

As committed educators, we often spend inordinate amounts of time in dialogue about burning issues. We are quite extraordinary verbal processors, clarifying concerns and generating ideas. But then what? This is where the Data Teams structure comes into play. This is the "just do it" part of the process that separates data-focused teams from other grade-level, department, or team meetings. Action is the key word. We know what the problems are after following the process of examining the data, analyzing the strengths and challenges, identifying the goals and results desired, and (here's the key!) creating solutions to address the challenges and to build on the strengths. Focused, constructive, solution-oriented efforts to address the immediate needs are the outcome of the meeting. When we go back to the organized chaos of the classroom, what will we do differently to ensure that all students make real and significant progress in learning?

Teams must not waste time looking for a "silver bullet." Action research is much more effective and rewarding. Recognizing teacher expertise and building on and sharing existing skills, knowledge, and talents to find solutions to the instructional challenges identified by the data are effective ways to work. Remember—this is a short assessment cycle; therefore, choose a strategy that is shown to be effective (by research, by yourself, or by your colleague) and try it. As long as robust results indicators are in place to gauge adult actions (implementation, time, structures, and processes) and student results (assignments, assessments, quizzes, projects, and summaries), and capacity is added to change course as needed, you are engaged in a continuous-improvement cycle. Review, reflect, and act!

Rapid results are critical to the ongoing Data Teams process. The momentum and commitment to the collaborative work are maintained by setting short cycle goals and seeing the progress. Recently, we worked with a group of dedicated teachers in a small rural district. They were told by their administrator that they could have common planning time once a week (Friday afternoons from 2:45 to 3:45) for two months to try this "Data Teams thing." However, the administrator stipulated that if there were no results at the end of the two-month period, they would lose the collaborative time. Based on their data, they quickly identified a specific and critical content area and broke it down into one- to two-week units. Using simple and quick common formative assessments, they rolled up their sleeves and focused on how they would teach differently. They collaborated on strategies that had direct impact on student progress. In the first two weeks they saw extraordinary progress! Afraid that it might be a fluke, they continued using assessment data to monitor student progress while discussing and recording effective practices (adult "cause" data) that they determined had caused the jump in achievement. The remarkable results that continued over the two-month trial period astounded not only the principal but also the Data Teams members. Needless to say, the Data Teams' practices are now implemented across the entire school. What made the difference? The focus on adult actions.

"When teachers recognize that knowledge for improvements
is something they can generate, rather than something
that must be handed to them by so-called experts,
they are on a new processional trajectory.
They are on the way to building a true profession of teaching,

> *a profession in which members take responsibility*
> *for steady and lasting improvement.*
> *They are building a new culture of teaching."*
>

We don't need to continue to study the research to learn more—we need to act on what we know about learning. Structured collaboration to implement what we do know ensures instructional improvement that will guarantee improved student achievement.

Pfeffer and Sutton (2000, pp. 14–15) have become famous for preaching the "just do it!" philosophy. "…far from rocket science. They are, in fact, common sense … successful interventions rely more on implementation of simple knowledge than on creating new insight or discovering obscure or secret practice."

Collaboration Full Strength

> *"There is no greater power than a community*
> *discovering what it cares about."*
>
> MARGARET WHEATLEY, 2002, P. 166

"Mobilizing people to tackle tough problems" is simply good leadership practice, according to Heifetz (1994), but that mobilization is not accidental, casual, or occasional. It is intentional with absolute schedules and protocols. Meeting as a learning community can be a fun and interesting exercise, but surely and quickly it becomes inefficient and frustrating without a clear purpose, high expectations, and agreed-upon protocols and practice. For that reason, we long ago made rules for ourselves that we would never attend a meeting that did not have an agenda. Freewheeling conversation is entertaining and engaging, but not in schools where time is at a huge premium. Data Teams are about structured dialogue with action.

Consider short instructional cycles that have a common focus (standard, benchmark, or learning objective), use common assessments that have a formative purpose, and employ a common scoring guide. Periodically have a conversation about proficiency—what does it look like? How do our perceptions differ? How can we establish a common definition that can be shared with students? Share and analyze results, celebrate successes, and agree upon common challenges on which to focus. Develop, review, or revise short-cycle goals. Then, roll up your sleeves and have a rigorous and engaging dialogue about how to best teach. Eliminate some variables by choosing some common strategies. Agree upon indicators to monitor for fidelity of implementation. Teach! Assess! Watch for results.

Collaboration without both cause (adult) and effect (student) data we refer to as "collaboration light" (Schmoker, 2001). Casual collaboration without data has limited purpose and does not sustain and nourish student or adult learning. Discussion occurs and may be engaging—students are talked about, curriculum is reviewed, and assessments are discussed and put on the calendar (perhaps the merits of each may be "debated"), with a sprinkling of laments about "the state" and a sincere desire for improvement. In contrast, full-strength collaboration has a laser-like focus in which student papers are shared and moved around in piles, numbers and trends are dissected, and the dialogue is rich, rigorous, and engaging. Debates may rage but will be short-lived, as the focus is always on generating solutions for the identified challenges. This is not a time for competition; this is a time for honesty about challenges and uncertainties. This is where best practice develops.

Newly forming Data Teams must be prepared for resistance, missteps, mistakes, and even sabotage. If commitment to students and to results is the culture and the practice, don't underestimate the power of the team. Focus on exceptional teaching and the learning will follow. Don't waste precious time discussing anything that is not critical to the common focus. Remember—it is about all of you.

"True collaboration is a discipline—
a fragile, high-maintenance set of practices and attitudes
that need constant care and attention....
The schedule, the frequency, and the quality
of good team meetings need continuous care and attention."

MIKE SCHMOKER, 2001, P. 11

During the Data Teams meetings, continually monitor what is working for whom and what is not. Recognize and share the best of what you know and follow that with feedback. Adults need it, too! Feedback is a critical component of the Data Teams process. Review and reflection generate enormous dividends. Hefty dialogue about teaching practice is not necessarily comfortable and pleasant. This is where learning begins and where practice improves.

"You have to have the structure that allows people to get together.
You also have to have a culture that begins to break into this isolation of teaching,
to make it OK for people to be in each others' business

and talk about their common concerns about the work,
as opposed to doing only what they do in classrooms by themselves ...
[Y]ou have to have all the interpersonal skills necessary
to coax people out of their private sphere of practice into a collective practice."

RICHARD ELMORE, 2008 PP. 42–47

Data Teams: A Continuous Improvement Cycle

"The quality of teaching and student learning
can be significantly improved with professional expertise
that already resides within virtually every school."

DENNIS SPARKS, 2005, P. 84

A continuous improvement cycle must include a close examination of both cause and effect. The cycle of "plan, do, study, act" encourages the reflection that is necessary for true growth and improvement. A structured team that embraces the spirit of inquiry and has created an environment of transparency, safety, and trust is truly able to look at data openly.

In isolation, it is difficult to have a rich discussion of variables that affect data. While we may believe that an assessment is a true assessment of reading comprehension, problem solving, or understanding of the scientific method, we may actually be unintentionally assessing a whole host of other skills and experiences. For example, have students learned the appropriate strategies for taking the type of assessment that you have administered? Is the organization unfamiliar? Are they familiar with being assessed on critical thinking skills (e.g., "Why did the author…?)? Are they accustomed to different types of directions, and now they are being asked to make their own meaning? If language acquisition is an issue and language skills are not being assessed, are students given the opportunity to express their learning in alternative ways? These are only a few of the questions and issues that a truly collaborative Data Team would explore in its journey.

Only a fool would remain in the profession of education if he or she did not truly care about children. The work is psychologically, emotionally, physically, and cognitively demanding. Without the means and opportunity to collaborate and share, we have seen many well-meaning and potentially great educators leave the field for work that is more financially profitable and less emotionally demanding. Exit interviews with teachers leaving the profession often reveal distress that stems from isolation and lack of support. A key to teacher retention is providing them with the opportunity to work together to share challenges, receive support from colleagues, and increase their effectiveness. When the Data Teams process is implemented with fidelity, results create the evidence to ensure buy-in. Infused in the research of DuFour, DuFour, and Eaker (1998, 2008); Schmoker (2001); Reeves (2007); Sparks (2005); and Elmore (2005) is evidence supporting the practice of teacher collaboration with the focus on data. Support and celebrate the teams that are showing results. When teachers improve their practice and the results follow, the seeds of a collaborative culture are sown.

> *"A successful face-to-face team is more than collectively intelligent.*
> *It makes everyone work harder,*
> *think smarter and reach better conclusions*
> *than they would have on their own."*
>
> JAMES SUROWIECKI, 2004, P. 176

References

DuFour, R., R. DuFour, and R. Eaker. 1998, 2008. *Professional Learning Communities.* Bloomington, IN: Solution Tree.

Elmore, R. Spring 2005. "Building New Knowledge: School Improvement Requires New Knowledge, Not Just Good Will." *American Educator*, vol. 29, no. 1, pp. 20–27.

———. Interview. Spring 2008. "Practicing Professionals" by Tracy Crow. *Journal of Staff Development*, vol. 29, no. 2, pp. 42–47.

Fullan, M. 2008. *Six Secrets of Change.* San Francisco: Jossey-Bass, p. 13.

———. 1993. *Change Forces—Probing the Depths of Educational Reform.* Levittown, PA: The Falmer Press, Taylor & Francis, Inc.

Heifetz, R.1994. *Leadership Without Easy Answers*, Cambridge, MA: Belknap Publishers.

Hiebert, J., and J. Stigler. Fall 2004. "A World of Difference: Classrooms Abroad Provide Lessons in Teaching Math and Science." *Journal of Staff Development*, p. 15.

Pffefer, J., and R. Sutton. 2000. *The Knowing–Doing Gap.* Boston: Howard University Press, pp. 14–15.

Reeves, D. *Ahead of the Curve.* 2007. Bloomington, IN: Solution Tree.

Ruth, Babe. n.d. Quotation. Available at BrainyQuote.com: http://www.brainyquote.com/quotes/quotes/b/baberuth125974.html. Accessed April 26, 2010.

Schmoker, M. 2001. *Results Fieldbook.* Alexandria, VA: ASCD, p. 11.

Sparks, D. 2004. Quotation. In Mike Schmoker, *Phi Delta Kappan*, vol. 86, no. 1, p. 84.

————. 2005. *Leading for Results.* Thousand Oaks, CA: NSDC/Corwin Press.

Surowiecki, J. 2004. *The Wisdom of Crowds.* New York: Doubleday.

Wheatley, M. 2002. *Turning to One Another.* San Francisco: Berrett-Koehler, Inc.

Wise, A. 2004. "Teaching Teams: A 21st Century Paradigm for Organizing America's Schools." *Education Week,* vol. 24, no. 5, p. 43.

Wurtzel, J. 2007. "The Professional Personified." *Journal of Staff Development,* vol. 28, no. 4, p. 30.

Coaching
and Data Teams

A PRACTICAL LENS

> *"If ever a relationship could be characterized solely by a series of conversations, then the coaching relationship is it."*
>
> **ALLISON AND REEVES, 2009***

Dr. Elle Allison helps us to see the organic connection of Leadership Performance Coaching and the Data Teams process. She shows us the value of using a coach in the Data Teams process to listen, question, and inspire thought and action.

How do you use coaching in your Data Teams to provoke thought? Dr. Allison suggests using coaching when teachers return to their classrooms to implement strategies. **How can you replicate this practice to increase fidelity to the process?**

*Reeves, D., and Allison, E. 2010.*Renewal Coaching: Sustainable Change for Individuals and Organizations.* San Francisco, CA: Jossey-Bass, p. 181.

191

CHAPTER 11

Coaching and Data Teams

ELLE ALLISON, Ph.D.

"Imagine what could happen if more people in your district were known for how they support others to accomplish the most important goals of the organization."

Leadership Performance Coaching: A Vignette

Janine Hoke is one of those principals who participates in new learning experiences with an intention to wring every ounce of benefit out of every minute. She challenges herself with this question: Is this the "right" stuff, and, if it is, how will I apply it to make a difference for teaching and learning? Beginning in 2009, Hoke participated in professional development in Leadership Performance Coaching (LPC) for her district, Alief ISD, in Houston, Texas. She had gotten a taste of the power of coaching when she attended a district-sponsored overview session at the start of the school year. Hoke left that introductory session feeling like coaching was the "right stuff," and she made a commitment to learn more. Tracee Grigsby, supervisor of professional development for the Alief ISD, responded quickly to Hoke and other district leaders who expressed a desire to learn more. Grigsby scheduled a series of district-sponsored LPC training sessions and opened them up to district leaders at all levels. Not long into the seminars, Hoke saw that coaching not only would take her leadership to a new level, it could also make a difference for the instructional leadership team (ILT) at Miller Intermediate School regarding the ways in which team members influenced and supported classroom teachers—especially teachers who sought to accomplish breakthrough results with struggling students.

Not one to procrastinate or wait for perfection, Hoke immediately began sharing what she learned in her LPC training sessions with her ILT. The team readily embraced the concepts, and Hoke began to see that coaching could create a culture where empowering conversations to increase student success and build leadership at all levels within the faculty were regular practices. Knowing that deep implementation of coaching would require more staff members who were skilled in the ideas and processes, Hoke arranged for her assistant principals, who were important members of the ILT, to attend the LPC seminars as well. Now she had a growing cadre of people who could help her lead this initiative.

Simultaneous to preparing her ILT, Hoke also shared her plan with the rest of the faculty. In addition, Hoke began to use coaching more often in her leadership role as principal of her school. She observed the empowering impact of coaching on individual faculty members. Teachers who came to her for advice on how to approach a classroom issue or a student need found that when Hoke used a coaching mode, they discovered that they actually knew more about what to do than they had initially given themselves credit for. In an e-mail to Grigsby, Hoke said, "I am amazed at the immediate impact coaching has had on my position as a principal and as a person."

In order to leverage the positive momentum that LPC was beginning to gain in her school, Hoke and her ILT put their heads together to come up with an implementation plan. They knew that they wanted to use coaching as a way to support teachers during daily, job-embedded interactions to build leadership and to increase student achievement. Their strong commitment to using student achievement data as tools for identifying needs, determining classroom strategies, and measuring success guided them to link LPC to the Data Teams work of the grade-level Professional Learning Communities (PLCs). They decided to focus particularly on disaggregated data that showed a downward-trending achievement gap between African–American students and the whole group. According to Hoke:

> The next phase of this year's initiative is for the ILT to continue to grow leadership among classroom teachers within the school. Not only will ILT members work with teachers to groom them as future ILT members, they will also work with a specific teacher whose data from the state practice tests for Texas Assessment of Knowledge and Skills (TAKS) show gaps in African–American performance. The goal is to help teachers close gaps through improving instruction with excellent first-line instruction rather than looking for the "quick-fix solution" that has been given and implemented by *someone else.*

The teachers at Hoke's school found a natural fit between coaching and the Data Teams process of the PLCs. ILT members use coaching to support teachers during the time between the PLC meetings and to grow the next generation of instructional leaders. In addition, the teams themselves use a coaching approach to guide the data-driven conversations within their PLC meetings. Hoke and her team believe that coaching provides a missing link in the critical conversations that teachers have about student achievement. She says, "Our PLC sessions are data driven, but only holistically; they are focused on looking at enough individual student work, *asking the right questions*, and thinking on your own."

LPC makes conversations within Data Teams rich and reflective. It also enhances the conversations that teachers have with each other about the work that occurs between meetings, when it is easy to slip back into isolation and overlook the benefits of reflecting out loud on the implementation of instructional strategies and their effect on the students. Let's take a closer look at what makes coaching so powerful.

The Power of Coaching

Although definitions of coaching abound, credible and effective coaching approaches all reflect some form of these essential ideas:

- Coaching is a development process for individuals and teams. As such, coachees learn, change, and grow.

- Coaching is a process for accomplishing projects that are important to the coachee and to the goals of the organization.

- Use of a powerful conversational format allows coachees to uncover their wisdom about challenges and dilemmas that they face in their work.

- Coaching requires coachees to take action and to reflect on the impact of their actions.

- Coaching simultaneously develops coachees in the processes of doing important work, which builds the capacity to *do* important work.

Coaching Values

In order to work well, coaching is based on certain values. First and foremost is trust. Coachees must feel confident that the coaching relationship is one where anything can be brought up. Doubts, fears, perceived mistakes—all of these issues are natural whenever meaningful change is at stake. Coaches must be comfortable dealing with these emotions as part of the process and not judge the coachee for experiencing them. Second, coaches believe in the unique wisdom of others and are able to put aside their own urge to jump in and tell coachees what to do. Instead of racing to give solutions, coaches believe that coachees can generate ideas, gain new perspectives, and create options. Coaches trust the process of coaching, knowing that their job is to listen and ask questions so that coachees gain insight about what to do next and are inspired and self-empowered to go forth and do what needs to be done.

At The Leadership and Learning Center, LPC is described as ". . . a series of powerful conversations that develops leaders in the skills needed to communicate the vision, motivate and mobilize people, monitor indicators, and produce results through others. LPC is action oriented to achieve goals that matter." This description contains essential ideas about coaching and why it is an effective practice. However, coaching is so contextual that any definition falls short of conveying exactly how it makes a difference. What *is* clear is that coaching creates a sense of efficacy in others that empowers them to confidently take action in matters that are important to them.

What Makes Coaching So Powerful?

Organizations that support a coaching culture show visible support of reflective practice—a concept to which many systems give lip service and agree with in principle but then drop the ball when it comes to actually aligning policies and practices to support it. Coaching provides the time and space needed for reflective conversations that always lead to insight and action. It allows people to hear their own thoughts and make sense out of confusion.

Exhibit 11.1 juxtaposes what coaching is and is not and reveals in part what makes coaching powerful as a strategy for helping others in their development.

EXHIBIT 11.1 What LPC Is and Is Not	
What LPC is not:	**What LPC is:**
• Venting	• Solution finding
• Advice giving	• Listening and questioning
• One sided	• Reciprocal
• Passive	• Action orientated
• Always easy	• Renews and gives energy

Using coaching as an approach to find solutions and take action will override the temptation that some people feel to use coaching sessions to air complaints. This is not to say that coaching does not allow a person to vent frustrations; it does mean that venting is not the purpose of coaching.

Coaching is also not a framework for giving advice in the way that mentoring or consulting does. Coaching relies on the skills of listening and questioning that mediate the thinking of the persons being coached and allows them to uncover solutions that are responsive to the world in which they live and for which they must take responsibility. No matter how experienced they are, coaches cannot give advice from their past and expect it to fit the context of the person whom they are coaching. Moreover, the purpose of coaching is to instill efficacy and empowerment; advice giving will not achieve this effect.

Coaching is reciprocal. Both the coach and the coachee have an obligation to each other and to the organization to make the coaching process work well. The coach brings powerful processes that promote insight and lead to action. The coachee voices each thought and insight in order to expose them to the questions and comments presented by the coach. Both parties receive and respond to each other in the moment, and this reveals what is needed next.

Coaching always concludes with the coach asking the coachee, "What could you do? What will you do?" This means that each coaching session ends with a commitment to action. This also means that the next coaching session begins with some version of the question, "How did the actions to which you committed at the end of our last session go?"

If you have ever had the chance to coach or be coached, then you have no doubt experienced firsthand the internal struggle of thought that takes place on the way to a cognitive shift (Costa and Garmston, 2002). A cognitive shift is that moment when there suddenly comes an "a-ha" insight that loosens knots and reveals possibilities and solutions.

Coaching and Data Teams: A Complimentary Fit

"Data Teams adhere to continuous improvement cycles, examine patterns and trends, and establish specific time lines, roles, and responsibilities to facilitate analysis that results in action."

STEPHEN WHITE, BEYOND THE NUMBERS, 2005, P. 18

Coaching as a Way of Being in Data Teams

Data Teams certainly bring focus to teaching and learning for student achievement. A more subtle but equally imperative outcome of Data Teams is to increase the team's ability to understand The Leadership and Learning Matrix, shown in Exhibit 11.2. This matrix shows the powerful relationship between student achievement and the actions of leaders and teachers in the system and classroom (Reeves, 2006). The matrix also implies that teams take action to implement strong, frontline instruction and leadership strategies that are the *best* of what we know and do as education professionals, and that have a visible impact on student achievement.

EXHIBIT 11.2	The Leadership and Learning Matrix	

Effects/Results	**Lucky** High results, low understanding of antecedents Replication of success unlikely	**Leading** High results, high understanding of antecedents Replication of success likely
	Losing Ground Low results, low understanding of antecedents Replication of failure likely	**Learning** Low results, high understanding of antecedents Replication of mistakes unlikely

Antecedents/Cause (Adult Actions)

For a system to push its way through to the "Leading" quadrant on the matrix, it needs to connect cause and effect and take powerful actions known to lead to measurable outcomes for students. To continue to exist in the "Leadership" quadrant on the matrix, the system needs to continuously engage in conversations that illuminate how teaching, learning, and leadership are causing good results. However, this is not enough. The system also needs to understand *how* the system itself leverages energy toward these results and under which conditions the strategies would cease to work (Collins, 2009). Difficult conversations are required in order to remain in the "Leadership" quadrant of the matrix. A coaching approach turns these

EXHIBIT 11.3	How Coaching Adds Value to Grade-Level and Subject-Area Data Teams	

Steps in the Data Teams Process	What Teams Need	How Coaching Adds Value
Step 1: Collect and chart data	Conversations that surface the "right questions" to focus the team on student achievement priorities.	Coaching begins with the assumption that the team is out to improve a situation with which team members are dissatisfied and feel they can improve.
Step 2: Analyze strengths and obstacles	Norms and agreements to operate collaboratively and professionally in order to explore strengths and obstacles with genuine curiosity and vulnerability.	Data Teams face hard truths about the effect of teaching on student learning. Coaching cultures are founded on the idea that difficult issues can be brought up and discussed without judgment or scorn.
Step 3: Establish goals: set, review, revise	Courage and confidence to ask more of themselves and to achieve important, difficult goals.	Coaching is a support system for individuals and teams to accomplish results that cause them to stretch beyond where they have been currently performing.
Step 4: Determine instructional strategies	Insights about what the research says about the best approaches for improving teaching and learning and a commitment to achieve deep implementation of strategies that work.	Coaching leads coachees to thoroughly explore possible strategies from all angles and perspectives. Coaching questions take the team beyond the mechanics of implementing strategies and ask it to also consider the conditions under which the strategy will thrive or fail.
Step 5: Determine results indicators	Interdependency and personal accountability to the team to monitor progress and adjust actions to achieve early wins.	Coaching always leads to action and reflection about the impact of actions taken. With reflection come new insights and new decisions that lead to refinements and further action.

difficult conversations into empowering experiences. Exhibit 11.3 illustrates how a coaching approach adds value to each of the steps in the grade-level and subject-area Data Teams process. When teams embrace the assumptions and intent of coaching, a climate of support and empowerment permeates the Data Teams process that not only sets a tone for collaboration but also provides practical tools for talking with each other that make collaboration visible.

Numbers always have a story to tell, but in order to give voice to the numbers, members of Data Teams have to talk about them from multiple perspectives and with an open and innovative mind. Powerful coaching skills and approaches create conversation among teachers and leaders that give voice to data and help them understand the data within in a larger context. The basic coaching skills of *listening, understanding, questioning, and calling for action* provide teams with practical means to hold these conversations.

The Basics of Powerful Coaching Conversations

Coaching can take many forms, from formal agreements to informal networks of individuals who use coaching skills to support each other. People can also learn coaching skills in order to be better in any important relationship, including as members of Data Teams. Although formal coaching requires deeper knowledge, skill, and commitment, Data Team members who want to use coaching skills to "partner in thought" with another individual or team must master a few basics: listening, understanding, questioning in a way that provokes thought and possibility, and, finally, calling for action and resonating hope.

Listening

Lisa Sanders, M.D., author of *Every Patient Tells a Story: Medical Mysteries and the Art of Diagnosis* (2009), tells of two research studies that found that doctors allow patients to talk for an average of just twenty seconds before they interrupt. Some only allow three seconds. Moreover, the doctors in the study rarely, if ever, go back and ask patients to finish what they were saying. When the doctors and patients are interviewed separately after the conversation, 50 percent of the time they disagree about the purpose of the visit.

Although Sanders writes specifically about the troublesome communication habits of physicians, I venture to guess that the number of seconds that people are allowed to speak without interruption in *most* workplaces is not much more. Certainly, in all workplaces, conversations often end with neither party feeling understood.

Listening is the most important and the absolute first tool of coaching. Coaching requires an extraordinary type of listening, however, and it is not as easy as it sounds. In order to serve another person through coaching, you must listen with nothing added, nothing altered, nothing judged, and nothing resisted. This type of listening means no interruptions and no questions or comments until the person has completed what he or she wants to say. This type of listening is demanding, because it requires that the person doing the coaching is fully present and alert and cares about the other person and what this person has to say. The coach needs to let go of his or her urge to counsel and advise the person or team or share his or her own stories and random thoughts. Imagine the self-discipline this takes! When you remember and truly believe that coaching is a different way of being with someone, the payoff is always rewarding.

Listening with nothing added, nothing altered, nothing judged, and nothing resisted is uncanny in the way it works. When you listen long enough without interruption, and if you treat the conversation and the person as if they matter (Axtell, 2002), the effect on others is that they begin to uncover their wisdom. There are few things in the world that measure up to the experience of just listening to someone who is troubled or confused about something that matters to him or her, and watching the individual figure it out—simply by hearing him or herself talk about it out loud for the first time. I don't think that a more joyful moment exists for a coach than the moment when the persons or team members whom they are coaching say something along the lines of, "I really never understood the issue until I heard myself say it out loud just now! Thanks for helping me." When this happens, the coach smiles. The coach does not have to say a word for coaching to work its magic. The fact that someone listens at all makes all the difference in the world.

Understanding

The second coaching skill can be thought of as "understanding." Like every other coaching competency, this skill is quite active and demands mindfulness and intention in order to work. To perform "understanding," coaches must ask questions that:

- Clarify ambiguous or confusing statements
- Ask for relevant details without disrupting the speaker's train of thought
- Summarize, paraphrase, or translate what was said without changing meaning and intention.

These actions create understanding for both the coach and the coachee. Indeed, within the context of coaching, "understanding" is more than making sure that everyone is on the same page. For starters, the paraphrases, summaries, and clarifying and detail questions expressed by the coach lead the coachee to focus on what *might* matter most. How the coachee responds to the inquiries put forth offers the coach essential data about the current situation that allow the coach to mindfully select his or her next coaching move. This matters, because the last thing someone in "coaching mode" wants to do is ask irrelevant questions or make distracting comments that lead others down a path that is out of sync with the wisdom they possess. After all, empowering others to inspired action is the primary goal of coaching.

Questioning to Provoke Thought and Possibility

People who coach ask questions to inspire insight in the individual or team whom they are coaching. They do not ask questions to satisfy a personal or, heaven forbid, a voyeuristic "need to know." Nor do coaches ask questions in order to manipulate the coachee to come to a point of view that the coach feels is the "right" answer. When in coaching mode, the person in the coaching role is always in service of the coachee. Therefore, the questions asked in this phase of the powerful coaching conversation are open ended and are asked without judgment or the implication that the coach knows the "right" answer.

This is not to say that coaches must avoid asking provocative questions that ask the coachee to wrestle with the best concepts related to the issue at hand. I call these "thought leadership coaching questions." Thought leadership coaching questions still adhere to the purpose of coaching, which is to mediate extraordinary thinking for another person or team, but they also introduce theories and research that may stretch the coachee. Consider these examples of specific thought leadership coaching questions:

- How does the team feel about meeting at least twice per month to collaborate on lessons?

- How does the group resonate with Robert Marzano's research about the most effective classroom strategies?

- How do the standards for administrators shape the current evaluation system?

- What are the best lessons you've learned about using your body language to de-escalate hostile situations involving gangs?

- How do the people who report to you respond when you ask them for the data about their effectiveness? What is your level of confidence that they can obtain the data they need to communicate with you?

- What do you think about the current processes in place for the team to reference; for example, levels of specificity, best practice standards, access, and timeliness?

- What is your gut feeling about your communication plan on this? What questions are staff members asking?

Notice that these examples raise important ideas in teaching, learning, and leadership while retaining the qualities you expect from coaching questions. They are open ended to encourage inquiry as opposed to being a "right" answer, they are within the context of the coachee's concern, and they cause the coachee to draw on and reflect upon his or her experiences. These questions allow a person to hear and understand his or her own thoughts and, ultimately, to uncover the wisdom needed to move an important goal forward.

Calling for Action

According to the 2009 ICF Global Coaching Client Study, people are motivated to seek coaching over other forms of support when they want to accomplish important projects and goals. The report says, "A key differentiator for the industry is that coaching is seen as an 'action plan' rather than an exploratory process" (p. 3).

A powerful coaching conversation always leads to commitment to action. Without action, insight and inspiration have no place to go. Without action, frustration sets in, and before long, teams begin to feel that meeting together is a waste of time. As a development process, coaching has incredible built-in mechanisms that lead to positive change. Every coaching conversation ends with a commitment to action, and the next conversation begins with reflection on the results of those actions. The process leads to incremental yet profound awareness and implementation.

The Powerful Coaching Conversation Process

Coaching engages a conversation process specifically engineered to facilitate people and teams as they move from uncertainty to empowerment. All successful coaching approaches use a conversation process that includes these basic steps:

1. **Establishing the goal for the coaching session**: Coaches ask, "What are you facing in this important work, and what specifically would you like to be coached on today?"

2. **Listening to the story**: Coaches invite the person or team to tell them all about the issue. Coaches listen without interruption or judgment.

3. **Seeking mutual understanding (paraphrasing, summarizing, asking for clarification and details)**: This phase allows coaches to check their assumptions and ensure that they understand the coachee's situation. This phase also allows the coachee to "see" or "hear" his or her own thoughts, which reveals to the coaches even more about the situation.

4. **Mediating thinking and insights through open-ended questions**: Coaches ask questions that put relevant and important ideas on the table. Coaches invite coachees to wrestle with those ideas within the context of the issues they face in their work. This phase leads to "a-ha moments"—the uncovered new perspectives and new possibilities.

5. **Generating possibilities**: This is where brainstorming takes place. After the person or team has had some "a-ha moments," coaches leverages these insights into potential solutions by asking questions along the order of, "Now what seems possible? What could you do?"

6. **Committing to action**: Once new possibilities are on the table and have been explored for their value, coaches ask the person or team to commit to the best ones.

7. **Evaluating the session for effectiveness**: As the session ends, coaches ask the person or team members to provide feedback about whether or not they feel they are in a better place than they were when the session began.

Anyone who wants to support and influence others to engage in work that matters can use this powerful coaching conversation process.

In Between Data Team Meetings: Where Coaching Makes a Difference

"The research is undeniable—
verbal persuasion alone NEVER is sufficient;
any sustainable change requires follow-up and coaching."

DOUGLAS REEVES, 2007, P. 89

Data Teams processes are structured to help teams understand the best frontline teaching, learning, and leadership strategies and make a plan to implement and evaluate their impact. Here, in the implementation stage of the work of Data Teams, coaching is what makes the greatest difference.

School-level, grade-level, and subject-area Data Teams operate with the intent to engage in strategies known to make the greatest difference for students. Teams make these decisions with the best intentions to carry them out with efficiency and effectiveness. Yet, even with the best intentions, many teams feel overwhelmed, and the agreed-upon strategies and interventions either never get off the ground or are only partially implemented by a few intrepid people who cannot create enough momentum to overcome the complex reasons for inertia in the system. A coaching culture operates in favor of supporting teams in following through on their commitments and for sustaining energy that leads to important changes.

LPC is different from specific, instructional supervision coaching models in that it offers a broad structure for thinking about what is happening around the implementation of the strategies and actions that the Data Team members agreed to during their meeting. While instructional coaching supports teachers as they work with students and helps them think about how the strategies are working and how they can adjust and revise them, LPC supports teams and individuals to take action and be accountable for launching and sustaining the agreements of the team. LPC helps teams to think deeply about the systemic forces that are operating in a larger context. LPC and instructional coaching make for a powerful combination. While LPC helps teams interact in ways that promote implementation, follow-through, and sustainability, instructional coaching focuses on supporting teachers to effectively apply the strategies with students and allows them to revise strategies to meet the needs of specific students.

Imagine the impact that every single person can have in a school to improve student achievement when leaders coach classroom instructional coaches in their work and instructional coaches support teachers in delivering the best instruction to students. Imagine the impact when everyone in the organization engages in powerful conversations that make the best thinking visible to all.

The Coaching Leader:
To Coach and To Be Coached

Leaders who coach others discover a wonderful secret: The more you coach, the more you lead. But wait—there's more! Every time a leader uses coaching skills to draw out the insight and wisdom of the people they coach, they actively develop leadership in others, which, I might point out, deepens the collective capacity to do even more of the most important work in the organization and to reflect deeply on what will sustain the best of what works (Reeves and Allison, 2009). Leaders who coach create a win-win-win-win situation. Through coaching others, leaders gain precious time and focus, they create and support systemwide leadership development, and the organization realizes the most important goals that ultimately have the greatest impact on students. No, coaching is not a magic bullet; certainly, leaders must also supervise, mentor, consult, and advise. But when coaching *is* the most appropriate tool, the impact it has on individuals and the system is profound.

Leaders Who Coach

Leaders who coach their faculty and staff are astonished by the immediate impact it has on the people at work and in their lives. Consider these comments by two leaders who have embraced coaching as a leadership approach:

- Rinda Montgomery, assistant superintendent at North Central Education Service District in Oregon, says, "The Leadership Performance Coaching has enriched my personal and work life in many ways, and I feel so awed by the little miracles that result from trusting the process."

- Andy Velásquez, principal of Owens Intermediate School in Alief ISD in Houston, says, "It is amazing the number of mini coaching sessions I have had with staff members and colleagues. Coaching is truly a skill in which people use their voice to work through a situation as they are coached."

Coaching exemplifies the elements of highly effective professional development models. It is job embedded and focuses exclusively on the most important issues that people face in their work (Joyce and Showers, 1995). Because coaching is not telling or advising, it activates learning at extraordinarily high levels of cognitive rigor and leads to action. When coaching is combined with ample opportunities to learn and a culture that invites risk taking, experimentation, and discovery, coaching quickly becomes an essential tool of effective leaders. Consider these systemwide benefits that result when leaders embrace and use coaching:

- Retention of top talent and growth of promising leadership talent

- Increased commitment and ownership to initiatives by faculty and staff

- A culture that values reflection and is proactive

- Employees who are more independent

- More people who transmit positive emotions

- More people who listen well and who offer comments and questions to others to help them think through complexities and dilemmas

Leaders have many options for using coaching with the people with whom they work. The handiest models for a leader include the options of long-term project coaching, bookend coaching, and walkabout coaching.

Long-term project coaching involves a series of powerful conversations, all focused on the important matters that come up as the coachee works on a specific project. An important tool used in this type of coaching is the "hundred-day project." The hundred-day plan allows people to premeditate high-impact actions to move their project forward and to reflect on the impact of those actions.

Coachees recalibrate their hundred-day plan as "real life" unfolds around their project. Coaching conversations focus on how the project is going and on identifying the actions that will keep it moving in an effective direction.

Leaders can also engage in what I call bookend coaching. Bookend coaching is often a single coaching episode initiated by a faculty member who asks the leader to help him or her think through something that this individual is facing in the work environment. Leaders who engage in bookend coaching apply the entire powerful coaching conversation process, beginning with asking the other person or team to tell them what they wish to accomplish and ending with a commitment to specific action. Leaders bookend this conversation with a follow-up contact that asks the person or team members to share how the actions they took turned out.

The coaching format used most often by leaders is called "walkabout coaching" (Allison, 2008). Leaders use walkabout coaching when they are—you guessed it— walking around and about the people in the organization and stopping them to ask for advice and ideas. When leaders are engaged in walkabout coaching, they usually do not have time to engage in the entire powerful coaching conversation process. Instead, they use a few of the skills: listening, summarizing, perhaps using a metaphor to show that they understand, or asking just one insightful, open-ended question that leaves the other person feeling capable and empowered to do the work that matters to that individual.

Every time leaders choose to coach instead of give advice or give the "right" answer, they open a window and invite fresh thoughts into the room. Coaching is like taking a deep breath. In an era of "busyness," where many people feel overwhelmed and overworked, coaching provides time and space for renewal.

Leaders Who Are Coached

Master coach Paul Axtell (2008) tells us that organizations need to ask themselves, "To whom do your people go when they need generate ideas, get over upsets, and debrief events?" Leaders who allow themselves to be coached gain a performance edge. Research in 2009 from The Leadership and Learning Center revealed why leaders who allow themselves to be coached feel so strongly that it is an essential support system. Leaders who worked with a coach from The Leadership and Learning Center reported that they finished their project sooner and gained confidence in their ability to do their work. Not only did they grow in essential leadership skills, but their organization benefited directly from the projects on which they were coached (Allison, 2009).

Your Coaching Organization

This article began with an invitation to you to imagine more people in your organization who are known for how they support others in accomplishing the most important goals. We then explored coaching's application specifically to the work of Data Teams. Creating a coaching culture often begins with one leader who wants to accomplish remarkable goals. When these single leaders know they can gain a performance edge with a coach, they set an example for other leaders within the organization to do the same.

Melinda Boyle is director of curriculum in the Jefferson 509 district located in Madras, Oregon. When I first began coaching Boyle, she was director of human resources for her district and was committed to creating the best new teacher induction program possible. Her journey to coaching began when she participated in a Senior Leadership Institute. While at the institute, Boyle decided to add teacher action research to the new teacher induction program in her district. This decision required significant changes to the existing program and would impact large numbers of people. If ever she had a project that could benefit from working with a coach, this was it!

Over the course of the coaching experience, Boyle's insights led her to collaborate with colleagues in curriculum and professional development as well as with the mentor teachers themselves, who suggested that they link action research to the work of the grade-level Data Teams. At the end of the first year of the newly revised and renewed program, new teachers and their mentors celebrated with a data fair, where they displayed their projects and shared their results. Boyle is the sort of leader who is successful at most projects she undertakes. Through coaching, Boyle felt supported and empowered and had a chance to reflect on early wins. She says, "Every coaching conversations allows me to see the way forward, have confidence in taking the next step, and shows others that everything we want to do is possible."

The Power of Coaching

Data Teams gather with the intent to make a difference. They choose to collaborate, because they believe that together, they leverage their combined experience, knowledge, and skills to respond proactively to even the most challenging student needs. In collaborative groups, one person in a resonant state can positively ignite the entire group with hope, compassion, and mindfulness (Boyatzis and McKee, 2005). LPC is a powerful tool for transmitting the best thinking and optimism for accomplishing the most cherished goals of the organization.

References

Allison, E. Winter 2008. "Coaching Teachers for School Transformation." *Principal Matters,* no. 75.

———. 2009. "Introduction to Coaching." *The Reeves Report.* Available at http://www.leadandlearn.com/coaching. Retrieved April 10, 2010.

Axtell, P. 2002. *Coaching Skills: A Fundamental Approach for Supporting Others.* Moline, IL: Contextual Program Designs.

———. 2008. "Leadership Coaching Series." Training materials. Prior Lake, MN: Contextual Program Designs.

Boyatzis, R., and A. McKee. 2005. *Resonant Leadership.* Boston: Harvard Business School Press.

Boyle, Melinda. Personal communication, January 22, 2010.

Collins, J. 2009. *How the Mighty Fall: And Why Some Companies Never Give In.* New York: Harper Collins.

Costa, A.L., and R.J. Garmston. 2002. *Cognitive Coaching: A Foundation for Renaissance Schools.* Norwood, MA: Christopher–Gordon Publishers, Inc.

Joyce, B., and B. Showers. 1995. *Student Achievement Through Staff Development.* White Plains, NY: Longman.

Montgomery, Rinda. Personal communication, January 28, 2010.

PricewaterhouseCoopers (PWC). 2009. *ICF Global Coaching Client Study.* Available at http://www.coachfederation.org/research-education/.

Reeves, D.B. 2006. *The Learning Leader: How to Focus School Improvement for Better Results.* Alexandria, VA: ASCD.

———. October 2007. "Leading to Change: Coaching Myths and Realities." *Educational Leadership,* vol. 65, no. 2.

Reeves, D.B., and E. Allison. 2009. *Renewal Coaching: Sustainable Change for Individuals and Organizations.* San Francisco: Jossey-Bass.

Sanders, L. 2009. *Every Patient Tells a Story: Medical Mysteries and the Art of Diagnosis.* New York: Random House.

Velásquez, Andy. Personal communication, February 8, 2010.

White, S. 2005. *Beyond the Numbers.* Englewood, CO: Lead + Learn Press.